VULNERABILITY AND HUMAN RIGHTS

ESSAYS ON HUMAN RIGHTS

EDITED BY THOMAS CUSHMAN

This series features important new works by leading figures in the interdisciplinary field of human rights. Books in the series present provocative and powerful statements, theories, or views on contemporary issues in human rights. The aim of the series is to provide short, accessible works that will present new and original thinking in crystalline form and in a language accessible to a wide range of scholars, policymakers, students, and general readers. The series will include works by anthropologists, sociologists, philosophers, political scientists, and those working in the more traditional fields of human rights, including practitioners.

Thomas Cushman is Professor of Sociology at Wellesley College. He previously edited a series for The Pennsylvania State University Press titled Post-Communist Cultural Studies, in which a dozen volumes appeared. He is the founding editor of two journals, *Human Rights Review* and the *Journal of Human Rights*, and he now serves as Editor-at-Large for the latter. He is a Fellow of the Yale Center for Cultural Sociology.

OTHER TITLES FORTHCOMING:

Rhoda E. Howard-Hassmann, *The Second Great Transformation: Human Rights Leapfrogging in the Era of Globalization*

Keith Tester, *Humanitarianism and Modern Culture*

BRYAN S. TURNER

VULNER-ABILITY AND HUMAN RIGHTS

THE PENNSYLVANIA STATE UNIVERSITY PRESS
UNIVERSITY PARK, PENNSYLVANIA

Library of Congress Cataloging-in-Publication Data

Turner, Bryan S.
    Vulnerability and human rights / by Bryan S. Turner.
        p.   cm. — (Essays on human rights)
Includes bibliographical references and index.
ISBN 0-271-02923-4 (pbk. : alk. paper)
    1. Human rights—Philosophy.
    I. Title.
    II. Series.

JC571.T85 2006
323.01—dc22
2006012362

The Pennsylvania State University Press is a member of
the Association of American University Presses.

It is the policy of The Pennsylvania State University Press
to use acid-free paper. Publications on uncoated stock
satisfy the minimum requirements of American National
Standard for Information Sciences—Permanence of
Paper for Printed Library Material, ANSI Z39.48–1992.

CONTENTS

ACKNOWLEDGMENTS

This extended essay is based upon a series of lectures I gave at the University of Cambridge in the undergraduate program on citizenship and human rights. I am grateful to the students who took the Part IIB paper "Soc 6" and who, through their supervision papers, helped me formulate this thesis more clearly. My special thanks go to Darin Weinberg, who taught the paper with me and as a result played a major role in the formulation of these arguments. Other colleagues who have influenced this study of human rights include Gary Albrecht, Alex Dumas, Anthony Elliott, Mary Evans, Liam Gearon, James Hunter, Engin Isin, John Keane, Sue Kenny, Francesca R. Recchia Luciani, Michael Mann, Rhiannon Morgan, Darren O'Byrne, John O'Neill, Ruksana Patel, Roland Robertson, Colin Samson, and Sridhar Venkatapuram. Several Fellows of Fitzwilliam College, especially Peter Dickens and Emile Perreau-Saussine, offered valuable contributions to my understanding of social and political theory, and the Master, Brian Johnson, was enthusiastic in his support of my project. Jack Barbalet and Malcolm Waters provided trenchant criticism of my initial attempt to develop a view about frailty and human rights. Their criticisms forced me to rethink the argument. Anthony Woodiwiss has had an enduring influence on the central themes of this study as friend and colleague—an influence that started at the University of Essex in the late 1980s and has continued over two decades.

Aspects of this interpretation of human rights and vulnerability were originally explored in "The End(s) of Humanity," *The Hedgehog Review* 3, no. 2 (2001): 7–32; *Journal of Human Rights* 2, no. 2, a special issue on frailty and rights; "Biology, Vulnerability, and Politics," in *Debating Biology*, ed. Simon J. Williams, Lynda Birke, and Gillian A. Bendelow (London: Routledge, 2003), 271–82; and "Cosmopolitan Virtue," *Theory, Culture, and Society* 19, no. 1–2 (2002): 45–63. Issues in Chapter 5 were originally developed in my inaugural lecture as professor of sociology at the University of Cambridge in 2001, but it has been influenced by more recent work with Darin Weinberg on intellectual disabilities. Towards the end of writing this thesis, Fellows of the Asia Research Institute at the National University of Singapore reinforced my views about the universal relevance of human rights to multicultural societies.

Thomas Cushman and Sandy Thatcher of Penn State Press helped me convert a disorganized and fragmented manuscript into a coherent argument. John Torpey provided detailed criticism of the original manuscript and encouraged me to defend my view of multiculturalism and cosmopolitanism in the conclusion. I am responsible for any remaining flaws and infelicities.

Finally, let me express my gratitude to my wife, Eileen Richardson, for her care and companionship, without which this study would never have been completed.

CRIMES AGAINST HUMANITY

INTRODUCTION: SOCIOLOGY AND HUMAN RIGHTS

In this study of rights, the concepts of human vulnerability and institutional precariousness are employed both to grasp the importance of human rights and to defend their universalism. Vulnerability defines our humanity and is presented here as the common basis of human rights. The idea of our vulnerable human nature is closely associated with certain fundamental rights, such as the right to life. Indeed, the rights that support life, health, and reproduction are crucial to human rights as such. It is, however, difficult to enforce human rights, and hence we must explore the complex relationships among the state, the social rights of citizens, and the human rights of persons. Social institutions necessary for our survival are themselves fragile and precarious, and there is a complex interaction between our human frailty, institution building, and political or state power. (Any analysis of human rights raises questions central to the political philosophy of Thomas Hobbes: the sovereignty of the state, the social contract, and the universal rights of human beings.) Finally, because vulnerability has a close relationship to notions of suffering, on the one hand, and classical philosophical notions of virtue on the other, any study of rights needs to examine their relationship to morality and religion—that is, to the conditions that make human society possible. The sociology of human rights finds its intellectual place within this wider context.

In more detail, this extended essay is a sociological study of rights as they are inscribed in national forms of citizenship and human rights as they are manifested globally in legal declarations, conventions, and institutions. The tensions and contradictions between states, citizens, and human rights constitute much of the content of contemporary international dispute and conflict, and yet theories of human rights have often failed to consider the relationship between citizenship and human rights. Hans Joas in *War and Modernity* (2003, 23) has gone so far as to claim (correctly, in my view) that "the central conflict of values in this sphere today is the conflict between national sovereignty and the universalistic claims of human rights." Political commentaries on the relationships among human rights, citizenship, and state sovereignty are often both confused and contradictory. For example, the National Assembly of France declared in 1789 that "the natural and imprescriptible rights of man" were "liberty, property, security and resistance of oppression," but it went on to assert that "the nation is essentially the source of all sovereignty" and that no "individual or body of men" could be entitled to "any authority which is not expressly derived from it." While human rights are said to be innate and inalienable, social rights are created by states. These two contrasted ideas—the imprescriptible rights of human beings and the exclusive rights of citizens of sovereign nation-states—remain an important dilemma in any justification of rights. I argue that the protection offered by nation-states and national citizenship is declining, and yet the state and citizenship remain important for the enforcement of both social and human rights.

Consequently, this study of rights aims, among other things, to understand the differences between the social rights of citizens and individual human rights. Briefly, social rights are entitlements enjoyed by citizens and are enforced by courts within the national framework of a sovereign state. These social rights, which are typically related to corresponding duties, are what I shall call "contributory rights," because effective claims are associated with contributions that citizens have made to society through work, war (or a similar public duty), or parenting (Turner 2001b). A system of universal taxation and contributions to social services through income tax are obvious indications of social citizenship. As we will see in the course of this discussion, there are many problems with this definition, but it will suffice at this stage as a minimal account. By contrast, human rights are rights enjoyed by individuals by virtue of being human—and as a consequence of their shared vulnerability. Human rights are not necessarily connected to duties and they are not contributory. There is, for example, no corresponding system of taxation relating to the possession of human rights. There is as yet no formal declaration of human duties, although there has been much discussion of such obligations. The United Nations Educational, Scientific, and Cultural Organization (UNESCO) encouraged an initiative for a charter of the duties and responsibilities of states, but these initiatives have not yet had much practical consequence. Similarly, the United Nations Universal Declaration of Human Rights implies obligations, but they are not clearly or forcefully specified. While states enforce social rights, no sovereign power exists to enforce human rights uniformly at a global level. Human rights are universal, but it is often said that they are not "justiciable" and have no "correlativity" with duties.

Hannah Arendt presented an especially sharp criticism of "the Rights of Man" in *The Origins of Totalitarianism* (1951), where she observed that these inalienable rights were supposed to exist independently of any government, but once the rights of citizenship (with the support of a government) had been removed, there was no authority left to protect individuals as human beings. Human rights without the support of a sovereign state, she argued, are merely abstract claims that cannot be enforced. It appears to be impossible to define what they are or to show how they add much to the specific rights of citizens of national states. The right to rights only makes sense for people who are already members of a political community. Arendt concluded, bitterly and ironically, that these arguments were compatible with the views of conservatives like Edmund Burke, who had argued that an Englishman's rights were more secure and definite than the abstract rights of man.

Arendt's conclusions may be unduly pessimistic, and we probably have a better understanding of human rights half a century after she developed her criticisms. Nevertheless, in the United States, the notion of "civil rights" (for example, the creation of a universal franchise) is often used as if it were synonymous with "human rights," thus confusing the relationship between the rights of citizens and the rights of human beings. Alex de Waal (2003), for example, details how Martin Luther King Jr.'s vision of political freedom and involvement in the civil rights movement had a direct impact on President Kwame Nkrumah at the time of Ghana's independence in 1957. In this historical account, American civil rights are treated as human rights in a global, or at least international, framework. Notably, de Waal's elision implies either that the U.S. Constitution is in some sense a global legal framework or that globalization has made the distinction between human and social rights increasingly vague. This study of rights explores this ambiguity between the claims of citizens and the "rights of man." Understanding the relationship between citizenship and human rights is key to understanding the precariousness of political and legal institutions, such as the rule of law, in many conflict-ridden societies.

This intellectually fruitful tension between citizenship and human rights raises the question of how the enforcement of rights by sovereign nation-states relates to that by global institutions, institutions that attain legitimacy by virtue of international agreements and thus form an aspect of global governance. Although many theorists of human rights who are committed to globalization's potential benefits appear to welcome the erosion of national sovereignty, any historical overview of human rights in international and national politics brings us to the conclusion that effective human rights regimes actually require state stability and the institutionalization of national citizenship.

Human rights abuse is characteristically a product of state tyranny, dictatorship, and state failure as illustrated by civil war and anarchy. Again, a viable state acts as an important guarantor of rights. There is a valid argument, therefore, that the liberties of citizens and their social rights are better protected by their own national institutions than by external legal or political intervention. The often chaotic outcome of human rights interventions in East Timor and Kosovo might force us to the conclusion that any government that can provide its citizens with security, even with weak democracy, is preferable to a bad and ineffective government. (The ongoing internal security crises in Central Asia, Afghanistan, and Iraq might also be added to the list of failed, or at least problematic, interventions.) From a Hobbesian perspective, a strong state is required to enforce agreements between conflicting social groups. Another way of expressing this idea is to argue that we need to maintain a distinction between the social rights of citizens and the human rights of persons. The former are enforced by states; the latter are protected, but frequently inadequately enforced, by both nation-states and international institutions.

My primary intention, however, is to make a contribution to the development of the study of rights from the perspective of the sociology of the human body (Turner 1984). The analysis of rights has been predominantly the province of lawyers, philosophers, and political scientists. The contributions of anthropology and sociology to the study of rights have been, if anything, negative intellectual contributions. Anthropology and sociology have, over a long period, emphasized the cultural relativism of the notion of "the human." Because they have characteristically argued that "human rights" are Western and individualistic, they have been critical of any idea of universal rights.

One important distinction between sociology and politics is that political philosophy has primarily concerned itself with the question of justice, and hence the analysis of rights arises necessarily from an examination of the justice and legitimacy of political regimes. By contrast, sociology often portrays itself as "value neutral," and it does not raise normative questions about justice. Sociology approaches these normative issues indirectly—for example, from the study of inequality. The paradoxical consequence of this concentration on empirical studies of income inequality is that sociology typically does not study equality directly. Equality is merely the absence of inequality, and not an independent phenomenon, as it were. Normative debates about equality and justice get buried under empirical and descriptive analysis of inequality and injustice. Because anthropologists and sociologists have typically been either positivists or relativists, they have not developed an analysis of justice and rights, and therefore they have failed to engage with the most significant institutional revolution of the twentieth century—the growth of universal human rights.

While many rights activists find the philosophical problems relating to relativism irrelevant, the issue of cultural relativism carries major practical implications and consequences. If there is a right to intervene in the internal politics of other societies, then there is a problem relating to the legitimacy of human rights interventions. The right to intervene to prevent or to remove human rights abuses cannot be justified without some legitimate notion of universalism. The point of this essay is to challenge this legacy of positivism and relativism and to promote a sociological approach that starts with the idea of embodiment and human vulnerability. Human rights can be defined as universal principles, because human beings share a common ontology that is grounded in a shared vulnerability. Sociology is also well positioned to study the failure of institutions that exist to protect human vulnerability. In developing this perspective, the aim is to construct a normative sociology.

In the academic literature on rights, there has been a movement to reject the debate about universalism and cultural relativism as out of date and unnecessary. Obviously, the notion of natural rights as a universal framework has been under attack for decades. The rise of positivist law theories criticized the theological assumptions of the traditional notion of natural rights, and the distinction between nature and convention has been recognized in law since classical times. In the sociology of law, Max Weber was an important figure in establishing a positive notion of law as state command in sociology, and he was clearly hostile to any idea of universal law (Hunt 1978). Notions of universalism in the contemporary discussion of human rights are often attacked by activists as irrelevant and by social anthropologists as unfounded.

Michael Ignatieff has made an important contribution to the debate about relativism and universalism in *Human Rights as Politics and Idolatry* (2001). He aims to promote a minimalist liberal theory of human rights (via the notions of dignity and agency) that avoids any prolonged digression into metaphysical justifications of "human nature" as a basis for the universality of rights. More specifically, he wants to defend the political character of rights and to criticize any treatment of them in quasi-religious terms, that is, as idolatry. Human rights force us to adopt political positions because we are compelled to take sides in political conflicts, but adopting political positions does not mean that we have to convert the "advocacy revolution" into a modern idolatry. A minimalist liberal theory simply asserts the importance of human agency and dignity rather than offering what we might call a "thick" theory of common humanity. Such minimalist theories have been clearly influenced by Isaiah Berlin (1969), whose liberal philosophy defended the notion of "negative freedom" (that is, freedom from arbitrary constraint rather than freedom to develop one's personality through education). Berlin also rejected sociology because it appeared to promote social determinism over individual agency. These negative freedoms were inscribed in the foundational rights of the Declaration, and Berlin's version of liberalism became part of the West's ideological framework during the Cold War against communism. Communism, insofar as it adopted Marxism, also accepted social determinism over individual freedom of will as part of the scientific theory of historical materialism (Berlin 1978, 103).

In the second part of his argument, Ignatieff attacks cultural relativism, criticizing Western intellectuals and governments for their failure to condemn local or indigenous practices and customs that are undeniably cruel. He criticizes human rights activists for adopting cultural relativism, often implicitly, as the soft moral option. "Relativism," he avers, "is the invariable alibi of tyranny. There is no reason to apologize for the moral individualism at the heart of human rights discourse: it is precisely this that makes it attractive to dependent groups suffering exploitation or oppression" (Ignatieff 2001, 74–75). He does not, in fact, offer a direct intellectual argument against cultural relativism, but he makes a series of plausible assertions to defend his position. These are various.

First, it is important for activists to join forces with critical movements against, for example, patriarchal, theocratic, and authoritarian interpretations of Islamic belief and practice. Second, it is false to create a simple opposition between Western (individualistic) and Asian (collectivist) beliefs or traditions. Human rights culture has become local and is embedded in the activities of local nongovernmental organizations. International agencies demand adherence to human rights, but similar pressure also comes from local groups resisting oppression or exploitation. For instance, the women of Kabul who approach human rights agencies to defend their rights do not want to cease being Muslim wives and daughters. They are not interested in universalism, but merely want their basic rights to be (locally) respected. Women in Pakistan who work through local communities to protest "honor killings" are likewise not necessarily exercised by the philosophical question of relativism. Third, the universality of human rights does not imply universality of assent, because the existence of massive social and political inequality would make such agreements meaningless. In this sense, human rights doctrine is "a revolutionary creed, since it makes a radical demand of all human groups, that they serve the interests of the individuals who compose them" (Ignatieff 2001, 68). This assumption has the additional implication that, while human groups require some level of social consensus, the right of exit is fundamental to individual security. Rights of membership are important, but the right to leave a group may be more significant. Human rights in a global world are, increasingly, rights of social and geographical mobility. This was one crucial lesson of the fall of the Berlin Wall in 1989.

These are what we might call pragmatic arguments against relativism, but Ignatieff concludes his essay on idolatry with a much more substantial set of claims that essentially constitute a statement concerning human nature. Despite his liberal minimalism, Ignatieff comes close to offering an ontological argument in support of universalism. He recognizes the existence of certain "facts" about human beings: they feel pain, they have the capacity to recognize pain in others, and they are free to do good and avoid evil. They can and should be held accountable for their actions. These empirical facts are sufficient to lead us to the conclusion that human beings should be protected from cruelty. This conception of human capacities (moral empathy, conscience, and agency) is based on Berlin's liberal emphasis on rights and individual responsibilities, and they describe in minimal terms what is required for an individual to be a moral agent of any kind. Because agency and dignity are the foundation of human rights as such, these individual rights are prior to social and economic rights. Ignatieff concludes his second essay (2001, 95) with the general claim that "what is pain and humiliation for you is bound to be pain and humiliation for me." We should not stress the differences among human beings from the position of cultural relativism, but emphasize the common ground that unites individuals in an existential context of shared experiences of pain and humiliation. This capacity for suffering creates a significant basis for universalism.

While avoiding any systematic engagement with ontological arguments about human nature as a defense against cultural relativism, Ignatieff implicitly lays the foundations for a "thick" theory of rights in his observations about pain and humiliation. In this study I want to elaborate his argument in order to develop a robust defense of universalism from the perspective of a social ontology of human embodiment. There is a foundation to human rights—namely, our common vulnerability. Human beings experience pain and humiliation because they are vulnerable. While humans may not share a common culture, they are bound together by the risks and perturbations that arise from their vulnerability. Because we have a common ontological condition as vulnerable, intelligent beings, human happiness is diverse, but misery is common and uniform. This need for ontological security provides a strong moral argument against cultural relativism and offers an endorsement of rights claims for protection from suffering and indignity. While liberal theory is largely about the political dimension of human rights, ontological insecurity indicates a cluster of salient social and economic rights (to reproduce, to family life, to health care, to a clean environment and protection from pollution, and to protection from medical and technological exploitation) that are fundamentally connected with human embodiment. Torture, from this perspective, is the most fundamental denial of human rights.

A SOCIOLOGY OF RIGHTS

Why do we need a *sociology* of human rights? In the next chapter, I shall more fully develop this general approach to human rights through the twin concepts of vulnerability and precariousness, but at first sight, this argument might appear to be more psychological or individualistic than sociological. Yet such a depiction would be a misunderstanding of human vulnerability, and in particular, a misunderstanding of the claim that our vulnerability forces us into social dependency and social connectedness. We need social support and legal protection precisely because we cannot successfully respond to our vulnerability by individual acts undertaken in isolation. We need collective arrangements, including human rights protection.

The sociology of human rights is specifically concerned with the special importance of the International Covenant on Economic, Social and Cultural Rights (Woodiwiss 1998; 2003; 2005), namely, those rights that are directly connected with human need and the protection of human life. One possible criticism of sociology from a liberal philosophical perspective would be, therefore, that sociology neglects those individual rights that constitute our civil liberties. By emphasizing the importance of the human body and the concept of basic needs, it could be argued by way of criticism that it is not possible from these assumptions to derive those democratic rights that are associated with the conditions of political participation, such as that expressed in Article 20 (everyone has a right to freedom of peaceful assembly and association). This criticism is clearly potent, but it neglects the important connection between sickness and inequality—or more positively, the relationship between health and equality of income distribution. There is a well-established argument in the political economy of health that social and political participation in society is closely associated with health outcomes. One can therefore establish a connection between the enjoyment of democratic rights and the enjoyment of good health and demonstrate that these relationships are an important aspect of the theory of social capital (Turner 2004). Although the idea of vulnerability has a clear connection to the basic idea of a right to life, it can also provide an ontological foundation for rights relating to freedom, because there is an intimate connection between the right to life and the existence of the good society. This relationship is expressed in Article 3, which asserts that "everyone has the right to life, liberty and security of person."

Critics of sociology may remain skeptical about this argument, because they see a real clash between the idea of personal liberty (as the foundation of the enjoyment of rights as such) and the idea of social causation or determinism. Liberals such as Berlin and Ignatieff have both expressed the traditional criticism of sociology—that the deterministic picture of human beings rules out agency and hence rules out responsibility. Recognizing this connection between the scientific explanation of action by social causes and the need to defend human freedom and responsibility also informed Hannah Arendt's critique of sociology and the relationship between the social and the political. If human actions are determined, individuals cannot be held responsible for their actions and cannot be punished in a criminal process for their past actions. The most thoroughgoing expression of this argument was developed by Leo Strauss in *Natural Right and History* (1950), which explored the inability of Max Weber's sociological tradition to consider the role of justice in causal explanations. Weber was, in fact, aware of this problem and presented the standard sociological response to the free will argument in *The Methodology of the Social Sciences* (1949). The free will argument often assumes that human decisions and actions have to be random or without any causal antecedents if they are to be free. In this version of liberalism, free will literally means making choices without any preconditions. As a result, freedom appears to be arbitrary and irrational, because human freedom requires that it be unpredictable.

Weber (1949, 124–25) argued that we must distinguish between mere behavior and action, between behavior driven by instinct and goal-directed activities that involve our rational decision making. Our sense of subjective freedom is always greater in the case of actions that involve conscious decisions. Weber followed Immanuel Kant (1724–1804) in claiming that freedom was not simply spontaneous action but involved following moral rules, where we make choices between alternative courses of action. For example, Weber recognized that the German political elite was constrained by a variety of historical factors—the absence of an advanced middle class, the legacy of the aristocratic landowners (the Junkers), and the weak development of civil society—but complained bitterly that they consistently failed to take political responsibility for effective leadership, especially in the immediate aftermath of the First World War (Mommsen 1984). As a result, Germany was decisively outflanked by the parliamentary leadership of Britain and the United States. Awareness of the causal importance of social factors is never an excuse for indecision or lack of (political) responsibility.

In defense of causal arguments, a sociologist might claim that human beings always make decisions and take action in the context of a range of predetermining conditions, including individuals' socialization, social class position, and generation. Sociology examines how social structures create decision-making contexts within which people are either able to exercise agency or denied agency by circumstances outside their control or even knowledge. Sociologists do not have to characterize human beings as mechanical robots in order to defend the idea of causal determinacy, and they may also want to take a historical view of the nature of freedom. In fact, Berlin's opposition to sociology appears to have been shaped specifically by his antagonism toward the role of historical determinism in Marxist social science in communist Russia, but Karl Marx himself had a much more complex view of the relationship between "structure" and "agency," claiming famously that men make history but not under circumstances of their own choosing.

The problem of causal explanation in the social sciences is clearly more complex than I have expressed it here, but suffice it to say that acknowledging the causal importance of social structure does not rule out human responsibility, on the grounds that people can, in most circumstances, choose otherwise. This argument appears to have been the fundamental basis of Arendt's criticisms of Nazi officers and officials in *Responsibility and Judgment* (2003). These men could also have done otherwise.

There are arguments against sociology that are more profound than the liberal criticism of notions of causality. One argument against sociology is that, as a secular science, it has difficulty in contemplating the possible presence of evil in human societies, and yet monstrous forms of evil (in genocide, ethnic cleansing, and war rape) appear to be the very basis of human rights legislation. Here again Arendt's reflections on totalitarianism and the banality of evil in *Eichmann in Jerusalem* (1963) raise difficult questions, not just for sociology but for any social science that claims to offer causal explanations of human depravity. Atrocity appears to challenge conventional arguments in support of value neutrality. One example is the unresolved problem of finding adequate explanations for the rape of Nanking in December 1937 by Japanese forces without recourse to ethical (indeed theological) assumptions about human nature as an aspect of any adequate causal narrative. Cultural relativism, in whatever shape, appears to be exceptionally underdeveloped as a plausible approach to such questions.

If we take a longer historical view of the origins of rights as such, then the European Enlightenment has been a major factor in the acceptance of universal principles of rights, and it has also played a major part in the development of sociology. In rejecting cultural relativism, we can offer a defense of both the Enlightenment project and sociology against postmodernism, deconstruction, and various forms of pragmatism. In this respect, this sociological defense of human rights within a universal perspective is consistent with Jürgen Habermas's more general defense of Enlightenment modernity (1987). There is, of course, one major difference: I attempt to establish the idea of a human community based not on communicative rationality, but on our physical and moral vulnerability, and on the attendant risks to which such vulnerability leaves us prey.

FROM OLD TO NEW WARS

Warfare played a major role in social change in the twentieth century, including the social change that gave rise to an entitlements revolution. The great expansion of human rights legislation and culture over the last century has been a consequence of the mechanization of warfare, the growing number of civilian casualties in both civil and international wars, and the potential horrors of biological and chemical warfare. Historical accounts of the growth of human rights typically concentrate on the evolution of rights as such, but in this introduction

I want also to consider the rise of the notion of "humanity" as itself a result of the globalization of the technical means of violence. We need to understand the growth of human rights against this broader historical context. In *Crimes Against Humanity*, Geoffrey Robertson (2002) traces the historical origins of human rights back to the Second Lateran Council's decision in 1139 to prohibit the use of the crossbow in wars between Christians. This historical interpretation is interesting in drawing attention to a mechanical instrument of warfare (the crossbow) and its use within a community (of Christians).

Any date for the historical origins of these rights will always be somewhat arbitrary, but the impact of military technology on civilian or unarmed populations in modern warfare can be deemed particularly relevant to understanding their growth. Martin Shaw in *War and Genocide* (2003) has examined the consequences of "organized killing" in modern society. His historical narrative opens with the Armenian genocide in 1915 and concludes with the Rwandan genocide in 1994. I want to push this discussion further back to the violent encounter between colonial settlement and aboriginal people. These colonial conflicts were features of the land rush that formed the modern world between 1650 and 1900. We might consider, for instance, the Wounded Knee Massacre of 1890, when between 150 and 300 men, women, and children of the Lakota Sioux people were killed by members of the U.S. Seventh Cavalry. This massacre, which involved the use of four Hotchkiss cannons that were capable of firing fifty two-pound explosive shells per minute, has all the hallmarks of what came subsequently to characterize twentieth-century violence: the mechanization of organized killing; revenge (for the Battle of the Little Bighorn); ethnic cleansing, whereby the Lakota were characterized in the *Nebraska State Journal* as murderous redskins; and the indiscriminate killing of women and children. The Lakota people's attempt to secure an apology from the U.S. government remains unsuccessful. The Congress drafted a formal apology only in 1990. In somewhat similar circumstances, in September 1898, British troops at Omdurman used Maxim guns and Martini-Henry rifles to kill some 10,000 Sudanese "dervishes" who were followers of the Mahdi on the banks of the Nile. (Approximately 48 British soldiers were lost.) For good measure, General Kitchener carried off the Mahdi's head in a kerosene can. Omdurman was to some extent a revenge for the massacre of General Gordon at Khartoum in 1885 by the Mahdi's forces. These colonial conflicts indicated the consequences of mechanization in modern warfare that were to be a feature of the twentieth century.

Colonialism is often considered to be an aspect of a civilizing mission to bring an Enlightenment culture to primitive cultures, and yet colonialism and slavery involved extraordinary brutality. Were men in tribal societies more or less violent? Violent combat in premodern societies and the use of torture have often been regarded as evidence of a lack of moral restraint. Historians and sociologists have frequently thought that the "primitive warrior" enjoyed the violence that he inflicted on the enemy. Extreme violence toward other human beings can be taken to indicate that outsiders were not regarded as human. Anthropological research suggests that preliterate societies did not have an expansive or comprehensive notion of humanity, but on the contrary, regarded themselves in exclusionary terms as "the People." Rituals that created a decisive sense of otherness often enclosed traditional communities. This ritualistic notion of an exclusive inside and outside world that separated "the People" from outsiders was often inscribed upon the body: tattoos and body piercing demarcated an ontologically separate community. Important notions of taboo and pollution describe the boundaries that separate human communities. Ritual cannibalism and head hunting, for instance, may be regarded as practices that decisively set the boundaries of the inside and the outside world. What and whom we are entitled through ritualized practices to enslave, to hunt, or to eat are powerful indicators of the border between the human and the nonhuman. This notion of the closed boundary of traditional or preliterate societies raises a question about civilizing processes. Norbert Elias has argued that modern societies require greater self-regulation and that aggression in modern warfare is increasingly impersonal. The transformation of the emotions is a significant feature of this history. In his discussion of "changes in aggressiveness," Elias (2000, 161–62) provides an important account of how violent passions in the early feudal period were slowly regulated as civilized forms of court society evolved.

Elias has undoubtedly produced one of the most influential theories of the transformation of violence in human societies in terms of the civilizing process. His argument is well known. It states that with the transformation of feudal society, the rise of bourgeois society, and the development of the modern state, interpersonal violence was increasingly regulated by social norms that emphasized self-restraint and personal discipline. The meaning of "civilization" in Elias's theory refers to the cultivation of individual moral restraint and the containment of aggression and passionate emotions in social interaction. The theory can be regarded as a moral pedagogy of the body in which raw passions and emotions are self-regulated through disciplinary regimes. The theory shows how developments in social institutions (such as the court, the state, and the bourgeois family) are important for and interact with the emotions and dispositions of individuals. Good manners and civilizing institutions are bound together in a dynamic historical process. In contemporary societies, social restraint and social order require the development of self-attention in which, through self-reflection (primarily through imagining what others think of us), we exercise self-surveillance and control (Barbalet 1998). In this sense, we can regard the theory as a historical psychoanalytic account of violent emotions within the sociological paradigm of the modern state. "Primitive man" in premodern societies was a more aggressive and emotional social being, but his rudimentary technology also meant that killing was a more inefficient and limited activity.

In modern societies, technology has greatly increased the capacity for killing; we can kill on a scale that earlier societies could not imagine. Modern men are also more likely to have grown up in societies where extreme violence toward outsiders is not a normal aspect of social training and development. The professional training of soldiers in a modern army means that they are socialized to kill without emotion, and in any case, hand-to-hand combat has become somewhat unusual in modern conflict, at least for professional soldiers. The preferred form of killing in modern warfare is now through aerial bombing, which minimizes casualties to armed forces while maximizing damage to an enemy. Bombing can typically take place without actually seeing the enemy. This technology obviously creates an emotional division between dropping "smart bombs" on an unknown enemy and the sense of personal, emotional combat (as described, for example, in the Icelandic sagas).

Elias's theory claims that, in terms of psychology, modern soldiers are not trained to be enthusiastic and passionate killers, but the evidence is very mixed. Brutality toward civilian populations in the fall of Berlin to Russian forces, genocide toward Armenians, the killing fields of Cambodia, the slaughter of women and children in Rwanda, and the eradication of villages in Darfur suggest that the "civilizing process" may be a fragile constraint over human behavior. Elias's theory attempts to say that modern man kills with less emotion. An alternative view is that modern societies, as opposed to modern people, are more violent than premodern societies. Technological change has made killing more efficient in modern societies, and wars are won by destroying civilian populations. This growing technological capacity has meant that the growth of the idea of "humanity" is a measure of actual inhumanity. In addition, it is possible to argue that there has been a "re-personalization" of killing in modern warfare. Mass warfare and universal conscription have largely disappeared, and the powerful commercial states—the United States, China, Japan, and the European powers—are increasingly integrated economically and diplomatically. At the same time, there has been an increase in local conflicts between rebel forces and states, which often involve ethnic cleansing and genocide. Conflicts in the former Yugoslavia, Chechnya, and central Africa frequently involve neighborhood killing, robbery, organized rape, and slavery, and they are characterized by extreme violence against the bodies of women and children. The aim often appears to be to induce as much fear and intimidation in civilian populations as possible. The methods involve camp rape, looting, pillaging, and hacking off limbs. Indeed, "violation of the body, with maximum pain, has become a common method of slaughter" (Shaw 2003, 138). It is possible to argue, following Elias, that the Nazi concentration camps involved an impersonal system of mass killing (Bauman 1989). Yet the theory of an evolutionary "civilizing process" is inadequate as a perspective on the personalized violence of combat in contemporary conflict zones. The growth of human rights institutions is a global response both to the mass killings of the Second World War and to the more localized, brutalized, personal killing of contemporary wars.

Technological developments in the twentieth century enhanced the capacity of states and their militaries to inflict systematic violence on civilian populations. Hiroshima and the Holocaust were both instances of the violent application of modern technology against civilians. In the second half of the twentieth century, however, there were important transformations of warfare. Herfried Münkler (2005) has identified three principal characteristics of new wars. First, while old wars were typically between states, new wars take place outside the parameters of the state, and this privatization of warfare is made possible by the reduced costs of armaments. For example, the Kalashnikov rifle is a relatively inexpensive but very effective weapon that has become a basic element in "small wars." The use of these cheap, portable weapons does not require a lengthy period of training and is not associated with traditional drill and discipline. Second, there is typically a significant asymmetry between the competing forces. Unlike the First World War, in which large armies engaged with each other on a battlefront over many years, in new wars, small armed forces (guerrillas or terrorists) create localized havoc, usually against civilians. Finally, Münkler perceives an "autonomization" of forms of violence that were once subordinated to and incorporated into a military system. One indication of this trend is that the divisions between criminal organization, insurgency, and warfare no longer exist. Just as terrorism is a privatization of the military, so the security forces that protect politicians and corporate leaders are themselves private, profitable agencies.

Three consequences of this privatization of warfare are especially relevant to human rights research and theory. The first is that modern warfare is characterized, in Münkler's terms, by short wars between states and long wars within societies. Second, there is a very close association between new wars and epidemics and starvation. Third, violence against women is escalating. In the Balkan wars up to fifty thousand women were raped, but in the Rwandan genocide, the figure was over a quarter of a million. Rape in new wars is designed to destroy communities by excluding young women from marriage and reproduction when their honor and self-esteem have been symbolically and physically destroyed. These three consequences all point to one conclusion: new wars make everyday life precarious, and human life becomes more vulnerable with social changes driven by a new economy of warfare based on the sex trade, drug control, and contraband. Child soldiers, cheap armaments, and the global drug trade have become key features of new wars in which military honor and discipline or rules of engagement play no part. While the new wars serve to underscore the argument that human vulnerability is the linking thread in human rights developments in the twentieth century, these new wars are obviously not subject to or regulated by human rights conventions. Wars between states are, in principle, subject to juridical interventions, but the possibility of controlling marauding warriors in Darfur or child soldiers in Myanmar is remote.

The study of war is thus an important, if depressing, sociological contribution to the analysis of human rights, but this descriptive account of the historical evolution of private wars in the modern period does not excuse sociologists from their failure to engage in or contribute to normative debates about human rights and the importance of the legal regulation of violence. The emphasis on technological and economic changes in warfare does not mean that cultural and social factors have played no role. Indeed, the value of Münkler's approach is that he recognizes the fact that the privatization of warfare also means that the traditional values of military discipline and respect for the conventions of war have collapsed. He perceives an important social relationship between the culture of new wars and the glamour with which Hollywood surrounds male violence in a postmodern culture. There is a sad irony in which the West, while condemning the mindless violence of terrorism, produces feature films that celebrate extreme violence as the hallmark of masculinity. We might call this "the Schwarzenegger factor." The cultural connections among Hollywood, new wars, and terrorism mean that intellectuals should seek to defend a higher order of values rather than pessimistically concluding that the defense of civilized life is a lost cause. The sociological imagination attempts to understand the empirical constraints on human behavior and the normative opportunities created by the rise of global human rights—to understand what makes everyday life precarious and what values may arise from our shared vulnerability. This interface of the empirical and the normative requires both comparative historical research and ethical analysis of the human condition.

CONCLUSION: COSMOPOLITANISM

Crimes against humanity have led to a greater awareness and acceptance of the notion of a common humanity. Treating other human beings as members of a common community is thus a radical historical development. I end this introduction by connecting these juridical developments with the debate about cosmopolitanism. Taking human rights seriously reflects an ethic of cosmopolitanism that can be associated with the Enlightenment. Specifically, the cosmopolitan philosophy of the German Enlightenment grew, in part, from the philosopher Gottfried Wilhelm Leibniz's fascination with Chinese civilization.

Although the European Enlightenment is most frequently associated with Kant, there is a strong case to date "the Age of Reason" with Leibniz. At first glance, Leibniz might appear to be an unlikely candidate as the father of human rights principles, and yet in my view he lays out the essential ethical ingredients for human rights as not only a juridical institution but also a shared culture. Leibniz is characteristically associated with the concept of "theodicy" (we live in the best of all possible worlds), which, his critics claim, provides a justification for violence and suffering in accepting the rationality of the world. Yet this interpretation fails to recognize the radical nature of his commitment to cosmopolitanism. Living in the best of all possible worlds meant, for Leibniz, not that all forms of injustice are part of a divine plan, but rather that a perfect world was one in which diversity had been fully developed and was reconciled with order. Because something (rather than nothing) exists, there is a principle of perfection, or the maximization of being. The astonishing diversity of cultures in the world is an aspect of this order-in-diversity principle. Leibniz wanted not only to recognize this diversity but also to celebrate it. Diversity does not entail disorder or chaos; it signifies ordered complexity.

Leibniz lived in a world where economic exchange was expanding people's horizons and bringing them into contact with other cultures. China was a topic of considerable interest, especially among Jesuit missionaries who had established contact with the imperial court. Leibniz argued that just as there was a commerce of exchange—that is, an exchange of commodities—so there ought to be a "commerce of light," in which ideas were exchanged between different societies. Leibniz, like Spinoza and Locke, supported tolerance toward other cultures, but he went even further to advocate "an imperative to learn from diversity . . . [and he] is the only prominent modern philosopher to take a serious interest in Europe's contact with other cultures" (Perkins 2004, 42). Even more remarkably, Leibniz recognized in his concept of the "monads" that this appreciation of the world's diversity was not simply from the perspective of an abstract mind separated from its body. Our relationship with the world is always through our embodiment. Human embodiment means that perceptions of the world are differentiated and limited. Yet embodiment, in creating differences, also creates the need for exchange, and it establishes the foundation for a commonality of human cultures. Cultural exchange is necessary, and it is made possible because our common embodiment forms the basis of a shared culture in which we can experience sympathy for other people. Moreover, we share, according to Leibniz, innate ideas that make communication possible. The intersection of these common realms allows sympathetic understanding while preserving the notion of infinite cultural diversity. In the best of all possible worlds, how does cross-cultural misunderstanding occur? Why is it the case that shared embodiment, common vulnerability, and innate ideas do not eradicate cultural disagreements? He argued that misunderstanding exists because human beings have freedom of action in recognizing or not recognizing others. Without this cognitive and moral autonomy, they could not act as moral agents. They would not, in fact, be able to live a virtuous life.

Leibniz's positive celebration establishes the foundation for modern cosmopolitanism, and within his hermeneutics, there is a more general recipe for "virtue ethics." In this notion, following Aristotle, the moral subject is at the core of the ethical life, and in order to flourish as ethical beings we need to cultivate and protect a set of virtues (Turner 2000). These virtues are ultimately grounded in human nature—and by this I mean simply that we are embodied. Hence virtue ethics attempts to take account of the psychological, sociological, and biological features of human beings. Virtue ethics constitutes the most appropriate ethical system for human rights as a set of legal injunctions. In placing Leibniz's cosmopolitanism at the core of virtue ethics, we can recognize that the components of cosmopolitan virtue are as follows: irony, both as a method and as a value, in order to achieve some emotional distance from our own culture; reflexivity with respect to other cultural values; skepticism toward the grand narratives of modernity; care for other cultures; and acceptance of the inevitability and value of cultural exchange.

Cosmopolitan virtue specifies a set of duties and responsibilities that correspond to human rights. The right to life carries with it a duty to care for others; the right to participate in the cultural life of the community has a corresponding duty to care for other cultures; and the right to free speech implies a duty to protect the exchange of light. From Leibniz's standpoint, we might argue that there is a duty to sustain cultural diversity and respect other cultures. These rights and duties can be derived from the need for cultural exchange and from the needs arising from human embodiment for sustenance, care, and dignity. This picture of life is an optimistic theodicy, and it is an open vision that needs defending in a world where the criticisms of multiculturalism and liberal optimism after 9/11 are gaining ground. (I develop such a defense in Chapters 3 and 7 of this study.)

While recognizing diversity, cosmopolitanism offers an important argument against relativism. How might we incorporate Leibniz's normative endorsement of cultural diversity into a sociological view of society? In his study of human misery, Barrington Moore (1970) argued that some weak version of cultural relativism was inevitable for social science, but that there is a well-developed consensus against tolerating human suffering. While there is a diversity of happiness, there is a unity of human misery. Thus a "general opposition to human suffering constitutes a standpoint that both transcends and unites different cultures and historical epochs" (Moore 1970, 11). If human rights exist to offer us protection from suffering, why not argue that there are universal human obligations to oppose human misery, to respect the cultures of other peoples, and to condemn governments that fail to protect human rights? Human rights legislation provides a formal juridical safety net against abuses, but the law needs an additional sociological buttress to have enduring effectiveness— that is, it needs a moral underpinning if legal contracts are to work effectively. Following Émile Durkheim's sociological criticisms of the theory of formal contractualism, society cannot exist on the basis of fear and coercion alone. There has to be an affective and moral basis to society, including such dispositions as care and respect.

Skepticism and a degree of distance from one's own culture can provide the basis for a duty of care and stewardship for other cultures. This description of cosmopolitan virtue ethics as a set of obligations flows from a recognition of the vulnerability of persons and the precariousness of institutions. It is intended to offer a stand against relativism and awaken the recognition of similarities between the prospect and problems of cosmopolitan understanding and an ecumenical commitment to dialogue with other cultures. The argument is not that contemporary cosmopolitanism can be simply a return to classical cosmopolitanism or religious universalism. Cosmopolitan irony is generally incompatible with these forms of nostalgia, because our contemporary dilemmas cannot be solved simply by a naive return to origins. The cosmopolitanism of the Stoics attempted to come to terms with the cultural diversity of classical times. Classical cosmopolitanism was a product of Roman imperialism, but contemporary globalization cannot be easily or effectively dominated or orchestrated by a single state. Contemporary cosmopolitanism follows from social changes that are associated with globalization. These changes include: the partial erosion of national sovereignty and the growth of postnational citizenship; the emergence of global markets, especially a global labor market, and a corresponding growth of diasporic communities; and cultural hybridity as an aspect of mainstream political life.

These global political communities require ironic and reflexive membership, if the modern world is to escape from the vicious cycle of ethnic conflict, revenge, and retribution. Cosmopolitan virtue may well turn out to be an ethic of exile for people who are migrants, and thus for people who are no longer attached to a permanent homeland.

VULNERABILITY AND SUFFERING

INTRODUCTION: VULNERABILITY, PRECARIOUSNESS, AND THE BODY

This study of human rights places the human body at the center of social and political theory, and it employs the notion of embodiment as a foundation for defending universal human rights. My argument is based on four fundamental philosophical assumptions: the vulnerability of human beings as embodied agents, the dependency of humans (especially during their early childhood development), the general reciprocity or interconnectedness of social life, and, finally, the precariousness of social institutions. The dialectical relationship between these four components becomes obvious when one thinks about the process of technological modernization. Within this dialectical balance of vulnerability, dependency, reciprocity, and precariousness, modern technologies—especially medical technology—have powerful and far-reaching implications, and they largely disrupt the relationships among the four components. If our embodiment is the real source of our common sociability, then changes to embodiment must have implications for vulnerability and interconnectedness. The new microbiological revolution in medical sciences, for example, holds out the promise of "the mirage of health" (Dubos 1960), including the prospect of "living forever." It is driven by a powerful commercial logic and has (largely unrecognized) military and security applications and implications that are problematic for human rights and democracy. New medical procedures such as therapeutic cloning, new reproductive technologies (NRTS), regenerative medicine, stem-cell applications, cryogenically frozen patients, fetal surgery, and organ transplants create the possibility of a medical utopia, but they also reinforce social divisions and inequalities, especially between rich and poor societies. This chapter raises two fundamental political questions. First, what are the proper ends of a political community? And does the current biotechnological revolution anticipate, following Michel Foucault (1970), the erasure of man?

Human beings are ontologically vulnerable and insecure, and their natural environment, doubtful. In order to protect themselves from the uncertainties of the everyday world, they must build social institutions (especially political, familial, and cultural institutions) that come to constitute what we call "society." We need trust in order to build companionship and friendship to provide us with means of mutual support. We need the creative force of ritual and the emotional ties of common festivals to renew social life and to build effective institutions, and we need the comforts of social institutions to fortify our individual existence. Because we are biologically vulnerable, we need to build political institutions to provide for our collective security. These institutions are themselves precarious, however, and cannot work without effective leadership, political wisdom, and good fortune to provide an enduring and reliable social environment. Rituals typically go wrong; social norms offer no firm blueprint for action. The guardians of social values—priests, academics, lawyers, and others—turn out to be open to corruption, mendacity, and self-interest. Yet the afflictions and uncertainties of everyday life also generate intersocietal patterns of dependency and connectedness, and in psychological terms, this shared world of risk and uncertainty results in sympathy, empathy, and trust, without which society would not possible. This contradictory and delicate balance between scarcity, solidarity, and security characterizes all social life. Such a theory of society embraces a set of Hobbesian assumptions, in which life itself is vulnerable—that is, nasty, brutish, and short. Yet it does not follow that we are forced to accept the individualistic assumptions of a Hobbesian social contract. Instead, human and social rights are juridical expressions of social solidarity, whose foundations rest in the common experience of vulnerability and precariousness.

As Pierre Bourdieu (2000) suggests in his *Pascalian Meditations,* the everyday use of our bodies leads us to acquire practical reason and to assume a habitus that expresses our tastes or preferences for various goods, including symbolic goods. In the process of this embodiment, we also develop a reflexive self that is always expressed *through* embodiment. Our selfhood is reflected in the peculiarities of our own embodiment; our eccentricity is articulated through these practices and our habitus. Two processes—embodiment and "enselfment"—express the idea that mind and body are never separated. Who we are is a social process that is always constructed in terms of a particular experience of embodiment. Suffering (a loss of dignity) and pain (a loss of comfort, which we need in order to feel secure and confident) are always intertwined, and so vulnerability is both a physical and spiritual condition. Finally, our experience of the everyday world involves a particular place, a location within which experiences of the body and of our dependency on other humans unfold. The notion of emplacement is taken from Martin Heidegger's account of *Being and Time* (1962), in which the concept *Dasein,* literally "there-being," specifies the temporality of being in space. Heidegger's philosophy of being-in-time conceptualized the inevitable contingency of human existence. Given that contingency, emplacement is crucial to our sense of identity, security, and continuity. Human rights abuses disconnect and destroy the conditions that make embodiment, enselfment, and emplacement possible. They typically involve some attack on the body through torture and deprivation, an assault on the dignity of the self through psychological threat, and some disruption to place through exclusion—imprisonment, deportation, seizure of land, or exile. (Elaine Scarry's *The Body in Pain* [1985] not only explains the relationship between political power and bodily afflictions but also details the consequences of the disconnection of self, body, and place through oppression and torture.)

The vulnerability of our everyday world is connected to a sociological understanding of the precarious nature of institutions. We need to comprehend the social world in terms of the relationship between the processes of embodiment and institutionalization. In sociological theory, "institutions" replace "instincts," because human beings do not have many ready-made instinctual responses to their environment. (Human instincts are malleable, minimal, and nonspecific.) Human society involves building an infinite number of "institutions," patterns of social interaction that are sustained by customs and sanctions—for example, courtship, the family, religion, rituals, eating patterns, sleeping arrangements, and political ceremonials. We create institutions to reduce our vulnerability and attain security, but these institutional patterns are always imperfect, inadequate, and precarious. Learning to live in society means learning how these institutions work or fail to work. This discussion of vulnerability and rights has to be located within a global social system, where the hybridity and fragmentation of culture bring into question our capacity to sustain solidarity in the everyday world.

The concept of vulnerability is derived from the Latin *vulnus*, or "wound." The idea of vulnerable humanity recognizes the obviously corporeal dimension of existence; it describes the condition of sentient, embodied creatures who are open to the dangers of their environment and are conscious of their precarious circumstances. This theme of human vulnerability clearly has strong religious connotations. In medieval religious practice and belief, veneration of the Passion was associated with meditation on the Seven Wounds of Christ. These palpable wounds served as evidence of Christ's humanity and suffering. Devotional meditations on Christ's suffering evolved eventually into the cult of the Sacred Heart, but perhaps the quintessential figure of religious suffering in medieval Christianity is the martyr Saint Sebastian, his body punctured by arrows. Our vulnerability is a traumatic wounding. It signifies the capacity to be open to wounding and to be open to the world. In modern usage, the notion of vulnerability has become, in one sense, more abstract: it refers to human openness to psychological harm, or moral damage, or spiritual threat. Increasingly, it refers to our ability to suffer psychologically, morally, and spiritually rather than to a physical capacity for pain from our exposure to the world.

As an aspect of human frailty, our ontological vulnerability includes the idea that human beings of necessity have an organic propensity to disease and sickness, that death and dying are inescapable, and that aging bodies are subject to impairment and disability. The human life cycle is characterized by its finite possibilities (and is thus inescapably tragic). Because of these conditions, human beings are involved in various relationships of dependency throughout the life cycle. Arnold Gehlen (1988) employed Nietzsche's aphorism—that we are "unfinished animals"—to develop an anthropological view of the frailty of human beings. Given their incompleteness, human beings need to build institutions to compensate, as it were, for their lack of instincts. Human beings are characterized by their "instinctual deprivation" and, as a result, they lack a stable structure within which to operate. They are defined by their "world openness," because they are not equipped instinctively for a specific environment. They have to build or construct their own social environment, which requires the building of institutions. Social institutions are thus the bridges between humans and their physical environment, and through these institutions human life becomes coherent, meaningful, and continuous (Berger and Kellner 1965). In filling the gap created by instinctual deprivation, institutions provide humans with psychological relief from the tensions generated by undirected instinctual drives.

The normative order *(nomos)* that human societies construct in response to the absence of specific functional instincts constitutes a social shelter or "sacred canopy" (Berger 1967). We can add to Berger's sociology of religion the idea that, as part of the protective environment of world-open human beings, legal institutions are fundamental in providing some degree of security in this precarious environment—and from this basic philosophical account of the ontological incompleteness of humans, we can derive the elementary forms of a juridical canopy in terms of the rule of law, habeas corpus, civil liberties, and rights. Human rights can be seen as a component of this protective juridical shield. Indeed, the social canopy is constructed of both rites (sacred institutions) and rights (legal devices of security).

INSTITUTION BUILDING

This construction of institutions is not necessarily a self-conscious or reflexive activity, and these social arrangements, in fact, must have a certain taken-for-granted character. Where such institutions become traditional, they are part of the taken-for-granted domain that makes social action possible. These traditional background assumptions give social life a certain degree of social stability and psychological security. Where the background is traditional, the foreground is, by contrast, occupied by more reflexive, practical, and conscious activities. Modernization, however, brings with it a process of deinstitutionalization—with the result that the background assumptions of social action become less reliable, more open to negotiation, and, increasingly, objects of reflection. The foreground expands accordingly, and life appears risky and precarious. The objective, sacred institutions of the past recede, and modern life becomes subjective, contingent, and uncertain.

Modernization involves increasingly flexible norms and institutions that change constantly in response to the speed and depth of social change itself. In fact, we live in a world of what Gehlen called "secondary institutions" or "quasi-institutions." These changes carry profound psychological consequences. Human beings in archaic societies had "character"—that is, a firm and definite psychological structure that corresponded to reliable background institutions. In modern societies, the individual becomes a "personality" living in a "lonely crowd" (Riesman 1950). People thus come to have personalities that are fluid and flexible, like the uncertain institutions in and by which they live. We can argue in these terms that the modernization of societies involves a "foregrounding" of cultural practices and institutions that can no longer be taken for granted. For example, with the modern medical science revolution and the development of NRTS, there has been a deinstitutionalization of familial and sexual life, in which societies have to become reflexive about reproduction and sexual identities. Gender identities and the circumstances of reproduction have to be constantly negotiated, and the traditional divisions between men and women are constantly reconfigured. Given this "individualization" of

sexual and familial relations, the rights and duties of parents are unclear. Modern societies have entered into "the normal chaos of love"
(Beck and Beck-Gernsheim 1995).

Social and political precariousness includes the inability of political
institutions to protect and secure the interests of individuals, the failure of social institutions to manage social change, the incapacity of
social institutions to reconcile the conflict of collective and individual
interests, and, finally, the difficulty of delivering equity in generational
exchanges. In human rights terms, the United Nations and international law are also characterized by precariousness. The UN has
proved, on many occasions, to be an ineffective and conservative institution that cannot offer security to marginal or brutalized communities. The reluctance to intervene in the Kosovo crisis, to define the
Darfur killing fields as a clear case of genocide, or to respond quickly
to the Niger famine in 2005 has meant that the brutal and cynical
destruction of life has gone on apace with no effective or robust response from the international community. It appears that societies
that do not occupy a significant part in Western foreign policy have no
means of protecting their own security. Human rights critics also
point out that while human rights criteria are readily applied to developing, non-Western societies, the United States can shrug off
criticism of its own failure to adhere to human rights standards
(Woodiwiss 2005). Put differently, there is a disjuncture between the
substantive rationality of human rights and the instrumental procedures and institutions that attempt to put them into practice. More
generally, social institutions have to be created and re-created over
time as they fail to respond adequately to social change. The process
of institutionalization tends by its very nature to be conservative and
cannot address the changing aspirations of new generations. The
transformation of charisma by routinization is a familiar aspect of
traditional societies, and tradition is subject to the constant impact of
both exogenous and endogenous change. In the modern economy,
management failures, hostile takeovers, predatory mergers, corporate
corruption, downsizing, organizational stress, inflation, currency instability, and restructuring are aspects of the precarious world of
global business. On a larger political canvas, the collapse of the com-

munist regime—as a consequence of the inability of a rigid bureaucratic system and a privileged elite to respond to economic and social
change—produced significant global instability in the 1990s and has
been at least one cause of the late twentieth-century spate of genocidal
conflict and ethnic cleansing. These civil conflicts and new wars in
the former Yugoslavia and Central Asia are classic illustrations of the
precariousness of modern societies.

Examples of institutional precariousness are relatively abundant:
the instability of global financial markets; the exposure of human populations to global disease through such conditions as HIV/AIDS and
avian flu; the instability of the natural environment through industrialization and pollution; the insecurity of orderly civil society through
the globalization of slavery, organized crime, and the narcotics trade.
Contemporary theories of social risk suggest that modern social systems cannot effectively resolve the complexities and contingencies of
social change, cultural diversity, environmental pollution, and urban
decay, and hence institutional precariousness is a consequence of
modernization and of globalized risk (Beck 2000). In turn, human
vulnerability is also increased, despite the important historical success
of public health movements, improvements in health care, and various spectacular breakthroughs in medical science. The dynamic and
dialectical relationship between institutional precariousness and ontological vulnerability drives the evolution of human rights legislation
and culture. Institutions need to be continuously repaired and rede-
signed, and human rights need to be constantly reviewed in the light
of their misapplication, misappropriation, and failures.

Both of these arguments—vulnerability and precariousness—
attempt to develop a contemporary version of Hobbes's theory of the
state without the limitations of a utilitarian and rational theory of a
social contract based on self-interest. Hobbes argued in *Leviathan* that
rational human beings with conflicting interests in a state of nature
would be in a condition of perpetual war. In order to protect themselves from mutual, endless slaughter, they create a state through a
social contract, which organizes society in the collective interest of
rational but antagonistic and competitive human beings. Furthermore, the institutions that humans create as protective or defensive

mechanisms have to be sufficiently powerful to regulate an individualistic market society, and as a consequence, the state can develop as a political agency that is necessarily a threat to human beings. For example, the state, which holds a monopoly over legalized violence, is both a guarantor of social security and, necessarily, an instrument of violence. The internationalization of human rights is intended to act as a check on state power and to guarantee that states respect the rights of their citizens. The problem lies in creating international agencies that can, morally and legally, coerce states.

This contradictory role of the state is the great paradox of human rights theory. As noted above, human rights abuses frequently proceed from failed states, from states that are unable or unwilling to protect their own citizens. Thomas Pogge, in his *World Poverty and Human Rights* (2002), has clearly demonstrated this. If a neighbor steals my car, I call for a policeman who attempts to apprehend the thief and to bring him to trial under criminal law. I feel angry and want the criminal to be punished. If the police force systematically robs a local populace and the state ignores this robbery, people feel that their human rights have been abused. Human rights abuses are not typically the result of the actions of criminal individuals, but of states and their agents. The Hobbesian paradox is that we need a strong state to protect us, but state power is often the cause of human rights failures. This paradox is part of what I suggest by the notion of "institutional precariousness."

Arguments about vulnerability and precariousness take on an economic dimension when we grasp the relationship between vulnerability and economic studies of the environment. In his *Entropy Law and the Economic Process* (1971), Nicholas Georgescu-Roegen argued that waste is an unavoidable aspect of the development process of modernization. Human beings inevitably deplete natural resources and create environmental pollution, and economic progress merely speeds up the inescapable exhaustion of the earth's natural resources. Georgescu-Roegen's theory showed that classical economics had neglected to study the problem of natural scarcity, thinking that technology and entrepreneurship could solve the Malthusian problem of population growth in relation to fixed assets. His economics of waste applied the biological ideas of Alfred Lotka (1925) to the accumulation of capital. Human beings rely on what Lotka called "exosomatic instruments" to develop the environment, unlike animals, which depend on "endosomatic instruments." In some respects, this is an old anthropological argument. Birds evolve wings to fly; human beings create airplanes. Wings, however, involve low-entropy solutions and do not deplete natural resources. Technological solutions, such as jet-propelled airplanes, are high-entropy recipes that use up finite energy. Because humans are somatically vulnerable, they develop high-entropy strategies that have the unfortunate consequence of creating a precarious environment. More importantly, the entropy law says that social conflict is inevitable because resources are scarce, humans degrade their environment, and they must compete within limited space. These Malthusian conditions of social conflict in modern times have been further exacerbated by the mechanization of violence and by the destabilizing impact of new wars. As a result, we can see social citizenship as an attempt to reduce conflict through (typically modest) income redistribution in the framework of the nation-state, and human rights act as conflict-reducing instruments between and within states.

SOME OBJECTIONS TO THE VULNERABILITY ARGUMENT

The argument that embodiment offers a fruitful basis for defending the universalism of human rights is partly grounded in the notion of the ubiquity of human misery and suffering. In 1850 Arthur Schopenhauer opened his essay *On the Suffering of the World* (2004) with the observation that every "individual misfortune, to be sure, seems an exceptional occurrence; but misfortune in general is the rule." While the study of misery and misfortune has been the stuff of philosophy and theology, there is little systematic study of these phenomena by sociologists. One exception is Barrington Moore, who argues in *Reflections on the Causes of Human Misery and upon Certain Proposals to Eliminate Them* (1970, 11) that "suffering is not a value in its own right. In this sense any form of suffering becomes a cost, and unnecessary suffering an odious cost. Similarly, general opposition to human suf-

fering constitutes a standpoint that both transcends and unites different cultures and historical epochs." A critic might object that suffering
is too variable in its cultural manifestations and too indefinite in its
meanings and local significance to provide such a common standpoint. What actually constitutes human suffering might well turn out
to be culturally specific. Those who take note of the cultural variability
of suffering have made similar arguments against a common standard
of disability. Although one could well accept this anthropological argument on the grounds that suffering involves essentially the devalua-
tion of a person as a consequence of accident, affliction, or torture,
pain is less variable. Whereas bankruptcy, for example, could involve
some degree of variable psychological suffering, a toothache is a toothache. If we claim that disability is a social condition—the loss of social
rights—and thus relative, we might argue that impairment is the underlying condition about which there is less political dispute. In short,
some conditions or states of affairs are less socially constructed than
others. Pain is less variable than suffering, if we regard the latter as
an indignity.

There is a strong argument, then, in favor of the existence of a
community of sentiment determined by the negative consequences of
pain and suffering, which are clear indicators of human vulnerability.
This notion that there can be cross-cultural understanding of the bond
of suffering was perfectly expressed in *The Merchant of Venice*, where
Shylock, in act 3, scene 1, offers a challenge to the standard forms of
Elizabethan anti-Semitism: "If you prick us, do we not bleed?" The
experience of vulnerability provides a norm for the assertion of a
human bond across generations and cultures, and this cross-cultural
characteristic of vulnerability presupposes the embodiment of the
human agent. A moral and political philosophy closely connected to
the notions of embodiment, suffering, and justice was powerfully developed in Mahatma Gandhi's struggle to control rising ethnic and
religious conflict between Muslims and Hindus in the context of In-
dian independence and postcolonial movements for democracy. The
centrality of health, diet, and sexuality—that is, a social theory of the
body—has been neglected in conventional accounts of Gandhi's life
(Alter 2000). The interweaving of concerns about landlessness, pov-

erty, and oppression in Gandhi's politics is especially pertinent to this discussion of vulnerability. In advocating dietary control and celibacy, Gandhi saw a clear relationship between the human body, the suffering of the peasantry, and the need for a democratic politics.

Gandhi's commitment to simplicity and nonviolence was deeply rooted in Hindu culture, but it also drew inspiration from Western (specifically German) naturopathy, which in turn entailed a critique of the rationalist and mechanistic assumptions of allopathic, Western, and colonial medicine. Gandhi articulated a government of the body, or control of the senses *(brahmacharya)*, in order to give individuals and social movements the power to resist colonial occupation and to transcend physical pollution and political corruption. Gandhi's philosophical defense of peaceful struggle provides further ammunition for the notion that vulnerability is the underlying foundation of respect for others. His openness to heterogeneous philosophical sources indicates that, with globalization, assumptions about local, autonomous cultures are questionable. We need therefore to understand this vulnerability against a background of global risks that in turn draw attention to the precarious nature of human institutions.

The vulnerability thesis can be further criticized because it is very relevant to some human rights, but not to others. The view of rights put forward by H. G. Wells and his colleagues in the 1930s is specifically pertinent to my position. Human beings are entitled, Wells argued, without any distinction of race or ethnicity, to nourishment, housing, and medical care to realize their full potential in physical and mental development (G. Robertson 2002, 23). In short, human beings have rights that are designed to protect them from their vulnerability—from the afflictions and perturbations to which we are subject as embodied creatures. It could be objected that this claim about vulnerability is relevant to the International Covenant on Economic, Social, and Cultural Rights, but it is not a convincing argument about the civil and political liberties in the Declaration. It may well be the case that the vulnerability argument will not form the basis of a claim about rights relating to individual freedoms of expression, privacy, and conscience.

There is, however, a clear relationship between poor socioeconomic conditions and health outcomes. The evidence from public health and epidemiological research demonstrates that human health is significantly influenced by income inequality and democratic participation in society. In particular, social capital (the investments that people make in society in terms of their membership in social clubs, groups, and associations) is a significant factor in morbidity and life expectancy (Turner 2004). It would not be difficult to show that human beings cannot successfully enjoy social rights to health care in societies that severely curtail civil and political liberties. For example, the spread of infectious disease with globalization is influenced by the democratic openness of different societies. The reluctance of China's political elite to respond transparently and quickly to the SARS outbreak—or the reluctance of some religiously conservative societies to recognize openly the impact of HIV/AIDS infection—shows that there are important connections among democracy, inequality, and health. Indeed, the authorities continue to harass nongovernmental organizations in China that have been assisting HIV/AIDS victims. Human Rights Watch reported in 2005 that Web sites providing information on the disease to homosexual men face closure under regulations prohibiting online pornography. These examples suggest that rights to health and well-being cannot be meaningfully separated from rights to democratic participation. One can forge links, therefore, between social conditions, health, and liberal political rights. While the argument about vulnerability might apply in the first instance to social rights, we can detect important connections between the enjoyment of social rights and access to individual rights or civil liberties as well.

This criticism of the vulnerability thesis might be summarized by claiming that it is limited by its inability to explain the individual rights of liberalism. Another criticism goes in almost the opposite direction: it questions whether there is any difference between human rights and animal rights. If my argument depends on the fact that human beings, as mammalian creatures, are vulnerable, then a critic might complain reasonably that one cannot distinguish between animal rights and human rights. Intelligent creatures that are not human are also vulnerable. Do dogs and dolphins have rights? Animal rights activists would probably want to claim that nonhuman higher-order animals are sentient, rational creatures. Some animals would thus enjoy the same right to rights that humans also claim. We certainly ascribe animal rights to certain sentient creatures, especially if they are closely associated with human societies, such as working dogs and horses. Some animals that appear to have an elementary communication system (effectively a language), such as dolphins, are thought to be eligible for protection. Yet unlike humans, animals cannot exercise these rights directly without our intervention. Animals cannot represent themselves. We might decide to protect animals as an aspect of a set of ecological rights that we have devised to protect our natural environment. Animal rights may thus be an aspect of a "green" or environmental politics that sees protecting animals as important for protecting human beings.

Giving rights to animals may not undermine the vulnerability argument, because animal rights are not unlike the rights enjoyed by other agents (children, the chronically sick, brain-dead patients, or the elderly) who cannot directly and actively enforce their own rights. Interestingly, we might also note that the dead have rights, in the sense that we feel an obligation to respect and honor the integrity of the dead by offering them "a decent burial," for example. The question of animal rights might therefore turn out to be part of a more complex philosophical problem about agency.

Yet another criticism, which I explore fully in a later chapter, is the medical technology paradox. The more medical science improves our health, the less vulnerable we are. Technological progress could make this vulnerability thesis historically specific. In principle, if we live longer, the relevance of human rights might diminish because we have become less vulnerable with technological advances. This paradox, though, helps me sharpen my argument, which is that we are human because we are vulnerable. We could only escape our vulnerability by ultimately escaping from our own humanity. Technological progress promises to create a post-human world in which, with medical progress, we might live forever. This criticism offers a very interesting argument, but there are two potentially important counterarguments. First, if we could increase our life expectancy, then we would live longer—but with higher rates of morbidity and disability.

The quantity of life might increase in years, but there would be a corresponding decline in its quality. A post-human world is a medical utopia that has all the negative features of a brave new world. Second, medical improvements in advanced societies are likely to increase the inequality between societies, creating a more unequal and insecure international order. In such a risk society, with increased human precariousness and decreased human vulnerability, the need for human rights protection would continue. The prospect of living forever might require us to inhabit, in Max Weber's (2002) pessimistic metaphor, a biological "iron cage" in which we exist courtesy of life-support machines.

VULNERABILITY, SYMPATHY, AND MORAL EDUCATION

The argument about vulnerability might survive these criticisms, but a skeptic might still pose another question: Why, if we are vulnerable, is the world so violent and the need for human rights protection so urgent and pressing? If sympathy stems from our vulnerability, why do marauding armies or guerrilla forces show such scant respect for life? Why are suicide bombers apparently not concerned by killing innocent civilians? Why do we inflict pain on others without any clear sense of remorse or guilt? A critic might accept the notion of vulnerability but still ask why people act so violently toward their neighbors, let alone strangers. These are old problems for philosophical arguments that want to show how sympathy can restrain violence. Perhaps acceptance of our own vulnerability and recognition of the rights of others fail when the interconnectedness and reciprocity of normal society are weakened or do not exist. This possibility suggests that the claims of vulnerability need some further argumentative support from the role of moral education. The mere existence of physical or psychological vulnerability by itself does not have sufficient force without some degree of training and socialization. Young children who are brought up in violent and traumatic circumstances will themselves be unable to recognize the plight of others, and hence their capacity for sympathy will be obscured and weakened. Child soldiers in African civil wars, who are often the products of violence and who may well be intoxicated with drugs, destroy villages, decimate families, and brutalize women without compunction. Violence provides them with resources and a certain level of power. In addition, there is probably a fundamental tendency to deny responsibility for the suffering we cause others. Our sympathy is offset by a capacity to reject the victim through a variety of psychological mechanisms (Cohen 2001). Various philosophical arguments have sought to advocate the importance of training in moral values as an antidote to cruelty and violence: to recognize moral duties, we need a moral vision through a sentimental training, a "moral education." An education in ethical standards that trains children to recognize the vulnerability of others will always be a partial solution, but it is an important aspect of human rights culture.

We can illustrate this position from the philosophical arguments of Richard Rorty. There are two major features to his account (1989) of rights—namely, sentiments and education. He places considerable emphasis on the importance of sympathy and affective attachment to other human beings. The sentimental attachment of human beings, through emotion and everyday companionship, provides the possibility for an argument about rights rather than some abstract claim about rationality. Human beings are primarily sentimental creatures, not rational philosophers. The next stage of his argument is probably the most significant: we should attempt to improve the world through sentimental education. Jean-Jacques Rousseau's educational theory of 1762 in *Émile* is particularly significant for Rorty's position. Through a system of education that would make people identify with other human beings rather than dismissing them as not truly human, we have an opportunity (however slim) to identify an appropriate framework within which to discuss rights at all. Rorty's optimistic belief is that we can make the world a better place by training our children into sympathy and concern for other human beings as themselves sentimental creatures. Rather than troubling ourselves with philosophical debates about morality's rational foundations, we should simply proceed with the business of trying to improve society through educational institutions and processes. The classics of literature are crucial to any sentimental education, as they contain the best that can be thought or felt. We can raise and enhance intersubjective sentiment through exposing our children and young people to the great traditions of literature and drama, wherein genuine moral dilemmas are explored systematically and sympathetically. The tragedies of Cambodia, Kosovo, and Darfur are more likely to be resolved in the long run by training children into a sympathetic appreciation of other people's problems and tragedies through instructing them in classical literature of the humanities. The moral issue behind human rights is, in essence, an issue of recognition—how to get human beings to recognize other human beings as creatures worthy of their respect, concern, and care. Rorty's argument about a sentimental education can be reformulated to make it compatible with the theme of vulnerability, but at the same time I want to avoid his relativist epistemology. The concepts of vulnerability and precariousness would thus sit easily with Rorty's own sense of the contingency of selfhood and a liberal community.

Following Rorty's view of compassion, we can derive a theory of human rights from certain aspects of feminist thought that take a critical view of the limitations of utilitarian accounts of reason and recognize sympathy and sentiment as critical alternatives to rational, instrumentalist theories of action. Rational human beings want their rights to be recognized, because they see in the plight of others their own (potential) misery. If aging is an inevitable process, we can all anticipate our own frailty, and in this context sympathy is crucial in deciding toward whom our moral concern might be directed. From a sociological perspective, sympathy derives from the fundamental experiences of social reciprocity in everyday life, particularly from the relationship between mother and child. The experience of suffering is an unavoidable outcome of human vulnerability. It is essentially a situation of the self's being threatened or destroyed from outside (through humiliation, for example). While suffering is variable, pain might be regarded as universal. This argument is closely related to a position developed in his essay "Private Irony and Liberal Hope," in which Rorty (1989, 88) argues that "the idea that we have an overriding obligation to diminish cruelty, to make human beings equal in respect of their liability to suffering, seems to take for granted that there is something within human beings which deserves respect and protection quite independently of the language they speak. It suggests that a non-linguistic ability, the ability to feel pain, is what is important, and that differences in the vocabulary are much less important."

While philosophical arguments about moral education are persuasive, they run up against severe sociological or empirical limitations. In a functioning society, the moral education of children and young adults may contribute to a culture that exhibits respect and care toward others, but Rorty's solutions are unlikely to survive easily in societies that have already broken down as a result of poverty, civil war, famine, and pestilence. Let us return once more to the Malthusian picture of new wars as described by Mary Kaldor (2001) and Herfried Münkler (2005). The entry of young children and teenagers into civil conflict and crime is a function of the structural impetus behind new wars—namely, high unemployment and the exclusion of uneducated and unskilled young people from the peace economy. Marginalized youth groups are not subject to the discipline of work, nor do they have any access to the world of consumption. They cannot form stable relationships that might result in normal family life, work, and reproduction. In this sense, they are not citizens but an underclass or surplus population. Ownership of a Kalashnikov gives them an opportunity to escape the boredom of street life, the deprivations of unemployment, and the humiliation of powerlessness. Civil conflict and gratuitous violence open up a fantasy world of masculine violence and domination. There is a peculiar interaction between Hollywood, consumer culture, and terrorism here: the warriors of the new wars, encouraged by violent videos, see themselves as Rambo-like figures of their local scene.

Moral education without economic reform, structural changes, and the rule of law will have little impact in such contexts. New wars are the consequence of the breakdown of civil society; the absence of employment opportunities; the collapse of family life; the impact of HIV/AIDS on employment, reproduction, and security; and the erosion of citizenship. The response to this crisis must include major economic changes, such as the cancellation of world debt and improvements in trade terms, legal changes such as the restoration of the rule of law and respect for human rights, and major political changes to combat corruption and injustice. If there is to be a response to ethnic cleansing, genocide, and new wars, it will have to embrace institutional changes rather than simply psychological or pedagogical reform of the individual.

One might conclude pessimistically that this global problem has no solution, because deeply entrenched interests—especially the economic interests of warlords and the illegal trade in drugs—sustain war and civil conflict. While this discussion may indeed suggest bleak conclusions, it does serve to reinforce the view that vulnerability and precariousness are dominant features of modern life, and that institutional solutions, including human rights, offer a more promising strategy than pedagogy. Moral education should not be discounted, but its success will follow and remain largely secondary to institutional reforms.

CONCLUSION: VIRTUE AND POLITICAL WISDOM

This account of vulnerability and precariousness is based on an attempt to recover the Aristotelian tradition of virtue ethics—in particular, an ethics that is closely connected with the everyday world's mundane needs. Virtue ethics recognizes that moral behavior requires character and that character is a consequence of training and cultivation. In this chapter, I have concluded by arguing that the benefits of virtue ethics are likely to depend on social and political strategies to protect civil society and civilized life. We suffer, and therefore we need institutions that will protect us. The world is precarious, and therefore we need to attend to institution building and the moral education of our children. Goodness is fragile; honorable people endure the contingencies of history and their own fate. Overcoming precariousness and vulnerability will always be subject to some degree of sheer luck and the fragility of goodness (Nussbaum 2001). Our political projects will never guarantee our security and cannot provide institutional arrangements that will survive indefinitely. Vulnerability gives some appropriate recognition of the importance of moral education, especially respect for other people and their cultures. This education is significant because it is an aspect of the creation of a common moral community within which emotions of sympathy can be cultivated and rewarded, but moral education must take place in a context of adequate civil and political institutions.

The experience of vulnerability teaches us political wisdom: respect for those institutions that have offered a modicum of security in the past. Alternative theories of politics tend to emphasize interest and the idea that rational actors will choose a social contract to protect their interests. These theories have an inevitably "thin" theory of society, one in which the unseen and beneficial consequences of individualism and competition hold the social order together. This interest-driven theory of the social contract and the market was notoriously summarized by the pronouncement of Margaret Thatcher, the former British prime minister, when she said that "there is no such thing as society. There are individual men and women, and there are families" (Keay 1987). Such a vision of social relations will never bind individuals and their families together as a viable community.

Rational choice theories that stress individual interest can only explain altruism as a calculating attitude, and they will describe such virtues as loyalty and compassion as yet other dimensions of self-interest. Yet without viable communities, there is no ultimate protection against vulnerability and precariousness. Human rights derive from vulnerability via the moral community, within which sympathy can be inculcated in the young. In this conclusion we can detect a useful and complementary relationship between descriptive sociology and normative philosophy. The sociology of war shows us that in many parts of the world, but particularly in central Africa, the Middle East, and parts of Asia, civil society has already broken down (often as a consequence of economic globalization). Human rights and international law offer some prospect, however limited, that the precariousness of life can be reduced so that educational strategies—Rorty's sentimental education—can begin to have relevance. The description of such war-torn communities implies a moral standpoint: that human beings ought to be protected from such suffering.

CULTURAL RIGHTS AND CRITICAL
RECOGNITION THEORY

INTRODUCTION: CULTURE AND IDENTITY

Cultural rights have become a crucial issue in contemporary politics. In an increasingly hybrid and multicultural global context, cultural identities are politically contested—and hence securing cultural rights is an important precondition for the enjoyment of other human rights. These cultural rights, however, may bear an uncomfortable relationship to the various identities that an individual might have as a consequence of diverse memberships in local communities, nation-states, transnational social movements, or global religions. With globalization, such diasporic communities proliferate, and cultural rights become more uncertain and contested. If culture defines identity, then culture is an important aspect of the basic right to have rights. That is, if human beings are to have the capacity to articulate their needs and interests, then cultural rights to language, religion, and identity are fundamental to the generic right to enjoy rights. Yet securing universal cultural rights is deeply problematic; it is difficult to justify them without confronting the problem of cultural relativism, and it is also difficult to know how these rights could be enforced.

National cultural rights in the context of heterogeneous, multicultural societies have themselves become problematic. We must therefore consider transnational claims to cultural rights from the perspective of universal human rights. While there are well-known philosophical and legal problems with any attempt to defend the idea of cultural rights, anthropological relativism can be criticized because it cannot adequately guide political strategies and policies. Cultural anthropology, in promoting cultural relativism, may be described as occupying a position of what I call "epistemological disinterest," because it cannot support political and legal judgments about ethics and politics. Epistemological disinterest ultimately spells political and ethical detachment. The notions of human vulnerability and critical recognition theory as a viable framework for human rights suggest an alternative position, however. This alternative strategy defends the idea of human vulnerability as an ontological paradigm for developing a universal defense of human rights via the notion of cultural rights. Recognition of the Other entails recognizing our mutual vulnerability, and this recognition opens up new possibilities for social solidarity.

The paradox of globalization is that, as states become more porous and sovereignty more problematic, ethnic or cultural identity takes on more importance as a criterion for defining communal membership. With global labor migration, the development of diasporic, transnational, and minority communities has raised new questions about political and cultural membership for which national citizenship often provides inflexible or inadequate solutions. As nation-states become more heterogeneous as a result of global migration and the deregulation of labor markets, more communities exist within nation-states as minorities, and the hegemony of traditional cultures and elites comes under direct or indirect attack. Traditional components of social identity and political membership—such as social class, occupational title, or trade-union affiliation—appear to recede in the face of the need to define oneself in terms of ethnic, religious, or other cultural markers. Creating, asserting, and defending cultural identity becomes an ever more prominent feature of secular politics, in which religious frameworks for identity formation become more urgent and assertive.

While modern politics is based on secularism and citizenship within the nation-state, in a post-national or transnational environment, religion has increasingly come to form the cornerstone of cultural identity, especially for minority communities. The emergence of post-communist societies illustrates the historical difficulty of suppressing cultural or religious identities in the name of secular politics. For example, in the Soviet Union, the state attempted to constrain national identities and religious affiliation by defining party membership as the principal form of individual attachment to society. Postcommunist ethnic wars have demonstrated, though, that the imposition of these political labels was relatively unsuccessful. In fact, class and citizenship in Stalin's Soviet Union were deeply marked by cultural forms of exclusion (Alexopoulos 2003). By contrast, in liberal democracies, cultural or religious identity is seen to be merely a personal preference and not a public identity. In a liberal market society, a person's identity was, in principle, determined by that individual's position in the market and associational relationship to the state. There have, of course, been significant variations within this Western model. The French republican tradition of *laïcité* regards the public arena as a secular space within which citizens are free to enjoy their liberty, and the state educational system attempts to insure that cultural differences remain irrelevant to participation in the public arena. Multicultural societies such as America, Australia, and New Zealand also feature a separation of church and state, but in those cases patriotism rather than republican secularity provided the social glue to bind different communities into a commonwealth.

Global migration, cultural hybridity, and transnational social movements have strained these arrangements, producing a set of contradictions between territorial membership (national citizenship), transnational identities, and human rights. The contemporary situation of minority Muslim communities in the West is one classic illustration of these political issues, but many diasporic Asian (specifically Chinese) business communities find themselves in similar circumstances. Social scientists have attempted to explain this global situation through a variety of theories providing new definitions of political membership. Notions of transnational, post-national, and flexible citizenship have been particularly influential in describing these identities (Ong 1999; 2004). Despite arguments in favor of flexible citizenship in the context of globalization, citizenship remains stubbornly tied to nation-states rather than supranational institutions.

Is this situation new? Historically, empires have had very diverse populations housed within an imperial framework that recognized some degree of religious, cultural, and legal pluralism. For example, the Ottoman Empire had a *millet* system that allowed people to enjoy some cultural differences under an elite-dominated common administration and bureaucracy, but because the elite was recruited from a variety of social groups across the empire (the so-called *devshirme* system), positions of power remained relatively open. The modern situation is different. National citizenship was produced by the growth of nation-states in the nineteenth century (and citizenship involves a territorially circumscribed set of rights), but cultural identities are now increasingly transnational and diverse. Democratization, rising expectations, and transnational social movements have encouraged people to express and articulate their rights. As a result, arrangements such as the *millet* system, which assumed a passive political subject, are no longer adequate. Many social scientists have criticized the inflation of expectations and the negative consequences of "rights talk," but they are an inevitable consequence of democratization. Nevertheless, many societies have found it difficult to recognize this political complexity and are reluctant to grant dual citizenship, let alone multiple forms of political membership.

Critics of policies that seek to recognize multiple identities have attacked educational strategies that embrace diversity through a multicultural curriculum. In *We Are All Multiculturalists Now* (Glazer 1997) and *Sovereignty under Challenge* (Montgomery and Glazer 2002), Nathan Glazer worries that multicultural education subverts historical truth and undermines national unity by the "Balkanization" of the American republic. Glazer and his generation originally believed that Americanization was unproblematic, because ethnic minorities would eventually be assimilated and benefit from growing economic prosperity. Migration could result in either a "melting pot" or a "salad bowl" of ethnic diversity, but the underlying pattern ran toward successful assimilation as migrants participated in the American dream of social mobility and prosperity. That initial optimism has been undermined, in Glazer's view, by the fact that the black community's progress appears to have come to an end in the 1970s. The attack on the Twin Towers (9/11) and the London bombings (7/7) have further challenged the viability of liberal multiculturalism (Joppke 2004). I shall address the contemporary disillusionment with multiculturalism in the final chapter of this volume, which discusses xenophobia. At this stage, suffice it to say that any discussion of cultural rights needs to take account of these tensions between national and transnational identities.

We can understand human rights as an aspect of the political problem of space and identity. National citizenship is based on the idea of a contributory right to participate in a political community that exercises sovereignty over a determinate territory. In Max Weber's famous definition, the modern state seeks a monopoly of force over a given territory and attempts to monopolize the attachment of its subjects. In short, it is the sovereign state. By contrast, human rights are rights enjoyed by humans *qua* humans within the global community whose sovereignty is expressed through fragile and fragmented legal agencies, such as international courts.

Cultural rights have become fundamental to human rights as a whole, because they attend to issues relating to personal identity and minority rights. They mediate between specific national citizenship rights and global legal entitlements. They are significant in defining what it is to be human; hence, peoples or individuals without secure cultural rights are highly vulnerable. Several articles in the Universal Declaration of Human Rights indicate their general importance: Article 15 (everyone has a right to a nationality); Article 19 (everyone has a right to freedom of opinion and expression); and Article 27 (everyone has the right to participate freely in the cultural life of the community). While Article 19 has been key to defending artistic and cultural expression in repressive regimes, Articles 15 and 27 address issues of identity and human dignity.

Underpinning these rights is the assumption that to enjoy a right, a person must be an autonomous, conscious, rational agent capable of communicative interaction. Human subjects have a capacity to understand and to articulate their interests. As members of humanity, they are also members of specific language communities. The fundamental cultural right is thus a right to a language. This observation may appear to be somewhat trite or obvious, but in a world of disappearing languages, many communities find themselves in a political context where their language is not recognized for official purposes. Without a recognized language, they are second-class citizens within somebody else's language community.

NATIONALISM AND CULTURAL RIGHTS

It appears to be relatively easy to define cultural rights within the framework of national citizenship. Cultural citizenship involves "cultural empowerment, namely the capacity to participate effectively, creatively and successfully within a national culture. Superficially such a form of citizenship would involve access to educational institutions, the appropriation of an appropriate 'living' language, the effective ownership of cultural identity through national citizenship and the capacity to hand on and transfer to future generations the richness of a national cultural heritage" (Turner 2001c, 12). Yet cultural citizenship is difficult to achieve in contemporary societies, because it is often hard to define what would constitute *the* national cultural heritage. British national culture has historically been deeply fragmented by class, dialect, region, and religion, and the political devolution of the United Kingdom created new opportunities for those historical differences to flourish. "Britishness" no longer adequately integrates English, Welsh, Scottish, and Northern Irish cultures into a single, more or less coherent political system. In the United States, patriotism does not completely incorporate every community from the mosaic of migrant groups. In this sense, America offers a kaleidoscope of cultures partially held together by patriotic populism, popular culture, religion, and the Constitution. Denominational and religious divisions between Catholic, Protestant, and Jew, for instance, have been historically overlaid by an American patriotic label that helps integrate new migrants into the wider society.

National identity has to be produced in a context where identities are fragmented by globalization. In the traditional terminology of sociology, citizenship building was necessarily a process of nation building. The creation of liberal institutions of citizenship in legal, political, and social terms also meant the construction of a national framework of membership within the nation-state—a process that dominated domestic politics in Europe and North America through much of the late eighteenth and nineteenth centuries. The national production of a framework for citizenship created a national "personality type" that transcended indigenous and local identities. Cultural citizenship was, specifically, the institutional framework within which national character was created. With the rise of nationalism, urban citizenship became increasingly connected with strong nationalistic cultures that sought greater domestic coherence and simultaneously organized negative images of outsiders. Nationalism does not necessarily assume an illiberal and intolerant form, but in the eighteenth and nineteenth centuries nationalism joined an imperial vision and eventually embraced racial ideologies that justified military supremacy over subordinate populations.

In the nineteenth century, cultural rights were an aspect of nation building and the hegemony of national cultures. The fragmentation of modern cultures and the growing hybridity of national traditions have confirmed the mood of cultural relativism and the postmodern turn among intellectuals. In this intellectual environment, it is difficult to defend the idea of universal cultural rights. Multiculturalism has served to reinforce anthropological relativism and a reluctance to be prescriptive about culture, tradition, and civilization. Indeed, "culture" in contemporary anthropological theory is often rejected as a reified, essential concept that cannot adequately describe cultural processes and practices. The creation of national citizenship ideally (but not necessarily empirically) presupposed a shared culture and a common language, often reinforced by a common religion. The continuity of these traditions further presupposed a common pedagogy and powerful educational institutions to buttress a common tradition. The fragmentation and commercialization of modern cultures raise difficult problems for the idea of a shared national culture within which citizens might enjoy common cultural rights. For some cultural critics, culture has become merely entertainment, involving the inevitable eradication of authentic, local content. The "McDonaldization" of culture has resulted in the "globalization of nothing," as standardized, commercial practices overwhelm indigenous traditions and tastes (Ritzer 2003).

ANTHROPOLOGY: JUDGMENT AND EPISTEMOLOGICAL DISINTEREST

Why dwell on the problem of *national* cultural rights in a discussion of the global importance of culture in human rights? The point of this introductory discussion has been to outline the specific difficulties of understanding rights as a component of human rights by first considering cultural rights within the framework of nation-states. Both the idea and ideal of global or transcultural cultural rights are clearly problematic. They endure the usual criticisms that are directed at human rights as a whole. First, there are jurisprudential issues. For example, cultural rights suffer from the lack of "correlativity." What duties might correlate to the rights to culture? There is also the question of enforcement. Are cultural rights justiciable? Moreover, there is a range of politico-legal questions about legal pluralism. Can the cultural rights of minority groups be recognized without undermining the state's sovereignty and the dominance of a single legal system? Can common law function as a single legal system, providing justice for dominant and subordinate communities without conflict and contradiction? Finally, the individualistic assumptions of Western notions of cultural rights and the endemic problem of cultural relativism raise anthropological issues. Cultural rights, as expressed for example in Article 19, emerged from the political struggles of artists and writers who wanted to be free to publish critical works. In particular, they grew out of the conflicts with the political elites in the Soviet Union and its satellites during the Cold War. They were intended to protect artists and writers like Václav Havel from political harassment and suppression—McCarthyism, Stalinism, fundamentalism, and so forth. Yet cultural rights are now central to questions of identity and dignity. They are not, I contend, merely superficial dimensions of the Cold War's legacy.

Anthropologists have taken the critical view that human rights legislation "essentializes" culture, making culture appear to be fixed and impermeable. This essentialism masks the fact that cultures are always evolving and changing. The notion of cultural rights often imperialistically imposes an organic, essential notion of culture on groups whose cultures and identities are fluid. Critical anthropology emphasizes the plasticity of culture as a construct against the essentialism expressed in organic analogies of culture, and it often condemns "cultural rights" as Western, individualistic, and imperialist. It claims that aboriginal societies, for example, have been typically defeated militarily by colonial powers, and the discourse of cultural rights actually serves as a method of cultural assimilation that does little to resolve fundamental sources of conflict, such as land rights. Instead of recognizing the resilient vitality of aboriginal cultural practices, the idea of "Culture" converts aboriginal society into a tourist site or an anthropological museum.

A recent collection of anthropological essays in *Culture and Rights* (Cowan, Dembour, and Wilson 2001) has provided a benchmark for anthropological responses to notions of human rights. I shall attend in particular to Heather Montgomery's "Imposing Rights?" which examines the case of child prostitution in Thailand. Her argument is that "childhood" is a Western category, whereas in Thailand, children are already employed in adult economic roles. They cannot be easily categorized as children according to the UN Convention on the Rights of the Child (1989). In rural Thailand, poverty forces households to depend on the income generated by child prostitution. Because parents send their children into prostitution to support the household, Western human rights intervention would drive a wedge between children and parents, destroy the household economy, and plunge the domestic unit into deeper poverty. We might disapprove of sex tourism, but our cultural categories (age grades, assumptions about responsibility, and Western sexual practices) should not be imposed on other cultures. This form of cultural relativism precludes taking decisive political intervention "from the outside," partly because such an intervention would destroy the tourist economy on which these people depend. Anthropology therefore involves a cultural critique of Western assumptions rather than a critical engagement with local practices, beliefs, and institutions. I have called this passive anthropological inquiry the academic politics of epistemological disinterest, because its apparent neutrality leaves the world as it is.

I argue, by contrast, that there is a common underpinning to human rights that recognizes the force of cultural relativism in anthropological research but asserts a minimalist ontology: we are all wounded creatures. The anthropological criticism of this argument might be that "vulnerability" is culturally variable and cannot, for example, be employed to suggest that children in Western societies are vulnerable rather like children in rural Thailand. Vulnerability may be defined in an elementary or minimal fashion, however. It is our propensity toward morbidity and inevitable mortality. A similar argument may be presented with respect to the vulnerability of children. While there may be no "children" in Thailand—a claim I happen to doubt—there are certainly people of a young age group who are vulnerable and require protection and respect.

The vulnerability thesis is intended to demonstrate that we have regard for other human beings because we share a common ontological openness. Vulnerability assumes the possibility of reciprocal sympathy. This emotional response is only possible, though, because an act of recognition precedes it. Human rights theory can in this respect benefit by incorporating G. W. F. Hegel's recognition ethics, which stipulates that an ethical relationship can only exist where there is a prior act of mutual recognition (Williams 1997). This recognition ethics is based on a principle of intersubjectivity in which mutual recognition must assume the freedom of individuals to enter into ethical relationships. If one party attempts to impose or command recognition, then freedom is replaced by domination. Human beings cannot therefore be adequately recognized as equally subject to moral and legal constraints if they are not recognized as human beings.

CRITICAL RECOGNITION THEORY

Care and respect for other people and their cultures cannot take place without a prior recognition of them as human beings. This feature of contemporary theory of ethics is referred to as "recognition ethics theory." The claim that an ethical relation requires recognition is derived from Hegel's analysis of the master and slave relationship. A master cannot receive recognition from a slave, because the slave is not in a position to give it freely. The master cannot recognize the slave because the slave appears as merely a thing. By contrast, love is the ideal context of recognition: two mutually attracted but free individuals offer each other perfect recognition. Hegel's recognition theory is not necessarily individualistic, because the same arguments apply to recognition between communities. Hegel's argument is sociological in the important sense that he accepted the fact that power and inequality are constraints on ethical recognition.

Mutual and free recognition are required if people are to be recognizable as moral agents. Rights in any case presuppose free, autonomous, self-conscious agents capable of rational choice, but life circumstances are unequal. The master-slave dialectic suggests that neither slave nor master can achieve mutual, intersubjective recognition, and without some degree of social equality there can be no ethical community. A system of rights and obligations, therefore, cannot function. Nancy Fraser (2001) expressed a similar argument when, deploring the separation between social theories of egalitarianism and philosophical commitments to recognition ethics, she asserted that redistribution must in fact be a condition of recognition. Social inequality or scarcity of resources undercuts the roots of solidarity or community, without which conscious, rational agency is difficult to realize. A variety of modern writers, such as Charles Taylor (1992), have appealed to recognition ethics as the baseline for the enjoyment of rights in multicultural societies. Without recognition of minority rights, no liberal democratic society can function, but recognition requires some material and legal changes to equalize the relationships between groups. It is also fundamental to the strategies by which aboriginal peoples may achieve social recognition and inclusion in modern societies. Although much human rights research has concentrated on the aboriginal peoples of North America and Australia, the complexity of recognizing aboriginal cultures has also been an issue in Japan, where, given the emphasis on national homogeneity, the indigenous Ainu—along with the Burakumin, Chinese, Koreans, Nikkeijin, and Okinawans—have found it difficult to secure rights.

There must be open channels of communication between the dominant host society (master) and subordinate minority groups (slave) for mutual recognition to emerge. Recognizing the rights of minorities must be the first step toward establishing a framework of rights. This critical notion can be modeled on Jürgen Habermas's communicative theory of democracy and normative order (Habermas 1997). An ideal speech situation must be in place for any dialogic recognition to take place. An ideal context for recognition requires a set of procedural rules: communication is not systematically or severely distorted by ideology; speakers have roughly equal opportunities to participate; there is no arbitrary closure of the communication; and there is no systematic domination over the speakers. Cultural rights require an open-ended opportunity for dialogue between host and minority, but also between anthropologists and their "subjects." These ideas have been extensively rehearsed in the literature on human rights (Deflem 1996; Deveaux 2000), but in this argument I intend to develop what I want to call a *critical* recognition theory. In recognition ethics, it is not enough simply to recognize the Other. There must be mutual opportunities for reflection and dialogue, and mutual recognition must also be able to incorporate mutual criticism.

Critical recognition theory can be seen as an application, therefore, of Habermas's theory of communicative rationality. Recognition involves recognition of the Other, but it does not necessarily require an acceptance of the Other's values and way of life *in toto*. Mutual recognition can take place without an overall consensus, provided there is trust and goodwill. We could imagine an ecumenical dialogue between Christian and Muslim communities that is based on mutual recognition, trust, and respect. Such recognition does not imply mutual acceptance of each other's theologies. Indeed, it might involve a highly critical dialogue: Muslims, for example, might argue that Christian trinitarianism is incompatible with a theology of monotheism; Christians might claim that Muslim theology lacks a viable sense of personal autonomy. Habermas's communicative notion of rationality implies that these theological debates might have no solution, at least in the short term. Recognition does not necessarily involve reconciliation of views. It may well be a drawn-out, acrimonious procedure. Recognition merely means that we respect the Other's arguments and, where possible, accept their intellectual force. It does not mean that we have to agree. There is, however, one further aspect of this example. It is also the case that some Christians—for example, Unitarians—would also agree with some Muslims that the trinitarian doctrine is ultimately incompatible with strict monotheism. And interestingly enough, some Muslims, including those known collectively as the Mu'tazila, would agree with some Christians that man's free will is difficult to formulate in a creed committed to strict monotheism.

This example suggests that critical recognition theory recognizes internal debates and internal contradictions in other cultures, while remaining skeptical about arguments and creeds from both sides of any dialogue. Critical recognition theory allows for mutual criticism; skepticism about one's own arguments, and skepticism toward the Other's position; failure to reach agreements, and hence ongoing debate; and, ultimately, a judgment or decision. As a consequence of this intercultural dialogue, it should be possible for both sides in principle to exercise some critical judgment toward one another. In terms of our example, it may be that Muslim scholars, having listened openly to many arguments, will make the judgment that Christian theology is ultimately incoherent. They may even conclude that Christian beliefs cannot be rationally held, and Christians might respond that religion depends on faith, not on reason. The role of judgment distinguishes critical recognition theory from anthropological descriptive relativism and from epistemological disinterest, because these positions rule out any judgment. They merely recognize at best that Christians and Muslims live in different cultures and therefore by different assumptions.

Two further aspects of critical recognition theory are worth noting. My account of the process of mutual recognition between two groups echoes pragmatist arguments against the possibility of discovering a final vocabulary (see Rorty 1989). A process of mutual recognition and mutual debate between two cultures is probably best carried out on the assumption that there are no conclusions, no final arbiters—and that judgments are always going to be tentative and open to revision. Disagreements between two groups need not be permanent. Second, cultural disagreements obviously test the boundaries of social membership, but the alternative is a society of closed and disengaged ghettoes between which there is, to use Leibniz's phrase, no commerce of light. The alternatives to dialogue, cultural exchange, respect for other cultures, and tolerance of sharp differences in belief do not look promising. The absence of critical recognition, debate, and cosmopolitanism will produce or sustain isolated, fragmented, fearful, and probably hostile communities living in a social space of separation and distrust. This situation appears to be characteristic of the existing relationships among ethnic communities in London and Paris, for example. The Bangladeshi community in London has little or no significant contact with the host community and is hermetically sealed from any outside cultural influence. Recent race riots on the beaches of Sydney suggest that even relatively successful multicultural societies, such as Australia, are not immune from ethnic conflict, copycat riots, and urban violence.

THE MASTER-SLAVE RELATIONSHIP

Recognition cannot take place between groups that are wholly unequal in terms of power. Kevin Bales, who in *Disposable People* (1999) has undertaken empirical studies of debt bondage (economic slavery) in India, argues that we must make an obvious distinction between the beliefs of slave owners and those of their slaves. Evil is in the eye of the beholder, in the sense that slave owners do not necessarily see their own activities in a negative light. The slave's loss of rights is seen as a consequence of the price the slaveholder pays to support the slave in terms of his basic needs. Slave ownership is often paternalistic and patriarchal. The slaves are the "children" of the slaveholder and they must be periodically chastised or punished like children. The slave owner comes to assume that he has a right, either God-given or justified by a superior civilization, to use and dispose of slaves as private property. It is, in short, a perfect illustration of the Hegelian master/

slave relationship that cannot permit mutual recognition. An essential feature of the master/slave relationship is that the master expends considerable time and effort to demonstrate, however implicitly, to the slave that slavery is not illegal and certainly not evil. Slavery is justified by reference to paternalistic norms or to the economic needs of the entire society. While much effort has gone into justifying slavery in India, Bales, reading through narrative accounts of ex-slaves in the 1930s, concluded that "none of them seem to have doubted the inherent wrongness of their enslavement" (Bales 2004, 62). A long history of slave rebellion in the British West Indies also appears to prove the point that the control of slaves depended ultimately on force and the threat of violence (Ferguson 2003, 79).

As a further illustration of modern slavery, Bales has turned his attention to sexual slavery in modern Thailand. He argues that girls are typically forced into prostitution through the brutality of a pimp who employs a mixture of violence and persuasion to control them. The girl will often be told that her parents will suffer economically if she does not comply. She will be told that prostitution is just a job. Occasionally the pimp will develop a relationship with the girl to reinforce her dependency. She will also be told that Thai values expect girls to be submissive and obedient. Bales goes on to argue that Thai Buddhist values encourage passivity, because suffering in this world is seen to be part of karmic debt. (I am not entirely convinced that this claim is fully warranted; there is also a Buddhist tradition of social justice and welfare that is derived from the good works of the first Buddhist monarch King Asoka [Ling 1973]. Clearly, Buddhism provides norms of passivity, but there are other alternatives as well.)

Following Bales's analysis, Montgomery's arguments that Thai prostitution is economically necessary and that there are culturally no children in Thailand provide further ideological ammunition for regarding sexual slavery as inevitable and not an evil practice. By contrast, human rights culture has, through globalization, extended the notion of evil to include all forms of slavery and challenges the normalization of child prostitution as an acceptable local practice. In the case of prostitution in Thailand, there must be opportunities for Thai communities to criticize the Western tourist industry for creating conditions that foster this abuse of women and children. There must be a critical inspection of the political economy of tourist prostitution rather than (or in addition to) anthropological descriptions of the ethnography of sex. Descriptive sociological research can therefore be directed toward normative policies, including social reforms of prostitution (Cabezas 2002). At the same time, sociologists might engage with internal debates in Thailand and elsewhere about the exploitative conditions of child pornography. Critical recognition would emerge out of this critical dialogue. Furthermore, critical dialogue must recognize the importance of an opt-out clause. Members of minority groups should not be compelled to accept their local customs and must have viable mechanisms to opt out (for example, by rejecting forced marriages or infibulation or child prostitution) just as members of host societies can opt out by migration (Kukathas 1992a; 1992b).

In these circumstances, an anthropological position of epistemological disinterest cannot be regarded as adequate. In the case of prostitution in Thailand or the status of women in Muslim societies, descriptive ethnography is incomplete, because it fails to recognize powerful internal critiques (for example, from Thai and Muslim feminists) against local or indigenous practices that make recognition difficult or impossible. Similar arguments apply to Islam. Critical recognition theory would take seriously the arguments of Muslim women such as the Sisters of Islam, who have challenged conservative Islamic interpretations of marriage and divorce in a context of increasing polygamy in Malaysia and elsewhere (Anwar 2001). Muslim feminists such as Leila Ahmed (1992) argue that many customary practices in Islam do not have Koranic authority and hence are not binding on orthodox women. Critical recognition theory would engage with internal Muslim critical debates and with Muslim criticisms of Western practices. This approach also takes seriously the criticisms of Western feminists who regard official Christian doctrine as often unsympathetic to women's spirituality.

This model of critical recognition pays attention to the fact that identities in modern societies are necessarily contested, given migration, multiculturalism, and globalization. Because it embraces these critical debates, it does not assume that the societies studied by anthropologists are based on a cultural consensus. Sexual practices in Thailand are the topic of massive internal debate. The status of women, the legitimacy of the headscarf, the nature of marriage, and the relationship between the sexes are also contested inside Islam (Haeri 1989). Critical recognition theory underpins the idea that mutual recognition will require mutual reflection and criticism. It thereby has the capacity to avoid both essentialism and relativism.

Of course, these arguments about the globalization of the discourse of rights have very different implications for the maintenance of cultural minorities in modern societies. For minority communities under siege from a hegemonic culture, protection of cultural rights is fundamental to maintaining the community. Cultural rights tend to be associated closely with the role of women (mothers) in the transmission of culture (language) across generations. Because familial and cultural continuity tend to be associated, sustaining traditional cultural rights can enforce conservative and restraining norms on women. Unlike Muslim men, Muslim women cannot easily marry out, especially in diasporic circumstances. The same arguments apply to Jewish communities, and indeed most forms of fundamentalism require the regulation of women in the interest of sustaining (or inventing) tradition. In the context of maintaining minority cultural rights in secular multicultural societies, the quest for cultural continuity may reinforce patriarchal authority within the family, resulting, for example, in arranged—if not forced—marriage. Although the opt-out clause is problematic in this context, it remains important if women's voices are to be allowed any expression. The sociological paradox is that in order to survive, minority cultures may need to regulate their women (by preventing out-marriage, for instance), but these forms of social closure also prevent or diminish the commerce of light that multiculturalism requires.

COSMOPOLITANISM, RECOGNITION, AND DIFFERENCE

Human rights are often criticized because they do not spell out any corresponding set of duties or obligations. The notion of cosmopolitan virtue can provide norms of responsibility toward other cultures, and these notions of recognition, respect, care, and responsibility can help us determine some duties that correspond to human rights. These "human duties" can be described under the umbrella notion of "cosmopolitan virtue."

Cosmopolitan virtue requires what we might call "methodological irony," because the ability to respect the Other requires a certain distance from one's own culture, namely, an ironic or disinterested distance. While that formulation of the problem is valid, there is an important addition: irony may only be possible once one already has an emotional commitment to a place. Patriotism in this sense may be not only compatible with irony, but its precondition as well. Irony may not be comfortable with intense nationalistic commitments, but patriotic love of a country, as formulated in republican philosophy, is compatible with both the capacity for ironic distance and regard for the Other (Bobbio and Viroli 2003). Perhaps irony without patriotism may be too neutral and thin to provide for affective identification and involvement with place and with politics.

This notion of ironic cosmopolitanism is intended to steer a course between two contrasted positions in the work of Maurizio Viroli and Martha Nussbaum. Against patriotism, Nussbaum has rejected the distinction between patriotism and nationalism, and she condemns those on the left who have argued that nationalism can be combined with universalism. In the interest of issues relating to international standards for quality of life—such as hunger, poverty, and ecological crises—she asserts that we must commit ourselves to a higher level of values (Nussbaum 2000). Her plea for cosmopolitanism is to establish an international framework for political emotions and social concerns. We must undertake a dramatic shift of allegiance from national citizenship to world citizenship, establish an educational strategy to promote understanding among other cultures, and accept a moral obligation to the rest of the world.

Nussbaum's argument is problematic partly because the creation of "citizens of the world" would require a global government to enforce rights and obligations. While I can, in principle, vote in a democratic government as a citizen of a state, I cannot currently enjoy many or any rights as a "global citizen." Here is one reason why the languages of human rights and of citizenship are not easily reconciled. Her sharp contrast between patriotism and cosmopolitanism is too severe, and it depends on what we mean by "patriotism." The danger with global cosmopolitanism is that it is too abstract and flat to carry conviction, whereas patriotism has the advantage of inculcating commitment to a living culture. But two aspects of her argument are very relevant to my account of cosmopolitan virtue. First, it appears to be self-evident that American patriotism, especially after 9/11, is not a promising basis for understanding other cultures, much less respecting them. Indeed, "American foreign policy, particularly with respect to foreign aid, ecology, and international trade, does little to address the moral scandals of modern times" (Bader 1999, 394). Second, most accounts of cultural relativism would imply that the contemporary cultural world is made up of a collection of tribes that have almost nothing in common. We need arguments that flesh out the commonalities of the human, especially social, experience. I use "flesh out" deliberately. We can make the cosmopolitan vision more convincing by arguing that the vulnerability of the human body provides the starting point for an account of human commonality as the basis for a cosmopolitan ethic.

One response to the growth of globalization and cultural hybridity was to embrace the so-called politics of identity in order to develop an ethical view (respect for difference) that is relevant to multiculturalism. Acceptance of cultural differences in multiculturalism does not, however, provide an effective basis for common purpose or communal integrity. The problem of cultural fragmentation and loss of solidarity has in recent years resulted in a volume of critical responses that attempt to create some revised grounds for universalism. Critics of the politics of difference have condemned left-wing politics as a betrayal of the Enlightenment's positive values. A politics of identity ends up as just another particularity—and leaves modern society exposed to "culture wars." The debate about cosmopolitanism raises the political question of whether citizenship can be de-territorialized. Skeptics of cosmopolitanism argue that a genuine democracy cannot be without territory, because love of country is a necessary prerequisite for pride in any democratic community. One learns political virtues within a definite spatial context, because respect for democracy cannot be easily divorced from commitment to a place. There is a parallel here between adherence to the faith of our forefathers and a global ecumenical regard for other religions. Can a committed believer have an ecumenical love of other world religions?

Cosmopolitanism does not mean that one does not have a country or a homeland, but one has to have a certain reflexive distance from that homeland. For this reason, cosmopolitan virtue requires methodological irony by which one can achieve some distance from the polity. If Nussbaum's plea for global civic education can work, then understanding other cultures presupposes that we could, in principle, treat our own culture disinterestedly as an object of inquiry. As such, cosmopolitan virtue also requires self-reflexivity with respect to both our own cultural context and other cultural values. Such an orientation of irony and reflexivity produces a humanistic skepticism toward the grand narratives of nationalism and modernization. Cosmopolitan irony would thus share much in common with the pragmatism of John Dewey and Richard Rorty, in that tolerance of the Other must start from a position of some uncertainty as to the ultimate authority of one's own culture. Cosmopolitanism assumes that there is doubt about the validity of any "final vocabulary," but cosmopolitan questioning of cultural authority is not equivalent to cultural relativism, especially what we may call "complacent relativism." Because cosmopolitanism engenders ironic self-reflection, it does not need a strong version of otherness, because its own identity is not profoundly shaped in conflict with others. It can offer a modest antidote to the thesis of an inevitable "clash of civilizations."

Skepticism and ironic distance from one's own tradition form the basis of an obligation of care and stewardship for other cultures. If cosmopolitans are urbanites, they have a special responsibility toward aboriginal cultures arising from an awareness of their precarious condition and hence acceptance of cultural hybridization. This description of cosmopolitan virtue—as a set of obligations—flows from a recognition of the vulnerability of persons and institutional precariousness with the globalization of culture. It aims to take a stand against relativism and to awaken an awareness of the similarities between cultures. It promotes understanding and an ecumenical commitment to dialogue with other cultures, especially religious cultures.

The argument, however, is not that contemporary cosmopolitanism is simply a return to classical cosmopolitanism or religious universalism. Cosmopolitan irony is generally incompatible with nostalgia, because it recognizes that our contemporary dilemmas cannot be solved simply by a naive return to origins. The cosmopolitanism of the Stoics attempted to come to terms with the cultural diversity of classical times, but contemporary cosmopolitanism is specifically a product of globalization and modernity. Classical cosmopolitanism was an inevitable product of Roman imperialism, but contemporary globalization cannot be easily or effectively dominated or orchestrated by a single political power. While American culture, especially popular and commercial culture, provides much of the content of contemporary commercial globalization, cultural exchange has also promoted the prominence of Japanese civilization worldwide. Similar arguments could be made for China in terms of Chinese cuisine, alternative medicine, and commerce. This view of global cultural exchange thus leads to a more complex and rewarding interpretation of the traditional understanding of Orientalism. Modern cosmopolitanism is a consequence of specific social changes associated with globalization. These changes include the partial erosion of national sovereignty and the growth of dual and multiple citizenship; the growth of global markets, especially a global labor market and an expansion of migrant labor seeking forms of quasi-citizenship; the growth of multiculturalism and cultural hybridity as aspects of mainstream contemporary political life; and the globalization of the politics of migrant communities, giving rise to diasporic cultures. These global political communities require ironic membership if the modern world is to escape from the vicious cycle of ethnic conflict, revenge, and retribution.

Cosmopolitan virtue is not designed to make us feel psychologically comfortable with cultural difference and diversity. Cosmopolitanism has a relationship to the traditional themes of homelessness in the theology of the Abrahamic faiths. As a consequence of their transgression, Adam and Eve were driven from their garden and forced to sweat and labor in an alien place. Homelessness was also central to Jewish themes of exile and exclusion, and it is generally shared by the world religions as an image of the vulnerability of human beings. If the body has been a metaphor of the human home, then homelessness expresses the fundamental spiritual alienation of human beings. The adventures of Odysseus provide an equally potent image of the tensions between the security of a dwelling place and the moral challenge of the journey. Odysseus's confrontation with diversity and his voyage home have been taken as a collective metaphor of human alienation.

This account of cosmopolitan virtue could be easily criticized as hopelessly naive and, even as a normative position, could be challenged for being out of touch with contemporary social and political realities. Cosmopolitans are criticized as rootless skeptics, uncommitted to place and local culture. In *Achieving Our Country*, Rorty (1998) condemns the liberal complacency of the superrich cosmopolitans who have turned their backs on the democratic American traditions of Dewey and Whitman. Cosmopolitanism could also be held to be elitist in the sense that the elite, in the comfort of their fortified mansions at a safe distance from other cultures and minority groups, can afford to be generous; slum dwellers cannot. Because these criticisms have considerable force, we can fruitfully turn to Montaigne to speak on behalf of contemporary cosmopolitanism. In the face of horrific civil war and religious violence, Montaigne called upon his fellow countrymen to exercise restraint and to adopt what he regarded as "feminine" virtues, lest they destroy themselves in a sea of blood. His disquisition on virtue and his reflections on cannibalism must also have appeared naive and elitist. My proposal for cosmopolitan virtue may be elitist, too, as it is addressed to precisely those powers responsible for resolving civil conflicts, war, and genocide in Chechnya, Bosnia, Cambodia, Kosovo, and Rwanda—those in power to exercise a set of obligations and moral leadership. Finally, there is a sociological argument behind this normative account of virtues. It is the sociological hope that, as global elites become more culturally diverse, geographically dispersed, and psychologically flexible, they will have to embrace global diversity more seriously and with greater determination.

This chapter has advanced an argument against cultural relativism in terms of a notion of human vulnerability. Some recent debates in the social sciences have also developed intellectual strategies that will permit us to develop universal propositions about rights while recognizing the importance of context. Charles Taylor (1999) argued that it is possible to have a global consensus on certain fundamental values (such as human rights), but the justification, application, and development of these values would depend on local traditions and customs. This process—by which the global adapts to the local—could be seen as an example of "glocalisation" (R. Robertson 1995). One illustration is the adoption of human rights culture and practices in Cambodia (Ledgerwood and Un 2003). While Cambodian Buddhist culture had little understanding of individual rights, its Theravada Buddhist values proved to be easily reconciled with human rights culture. Buddhist values of compassion, tolerance, and nonviolence provided a fertile framework for programs to promote human rights values in war-torn Cambodia. Leaders saw the crisis of the civil war as a consequence of the breakdown of morality, and they believed that respect for human rights could be achieved by the restoration of basic Buddhist precepts in the community.

CONCLUSION: VIRTUES AND DUTIES

Although human rights have been subject to major philosophical and legal criticisms, they represent an important evolution of rights beyond the sovereignty of the nation-state on which citizenship was originally constructed. Human rights overcome some of the limitations of citizenship, which is grounded in a contributory principle. They are not bound to the nation-state; they do not presuppose a contribution, because people *qua* human beings have rights; and finally, they address a range of issues related to identity in terms of culture, language, and heritage. One criticism of human rights is that there has been little effort to develop a notion of human duties. Through the notion of cosmopolitan virtue, it is possible to develop a theory of human obligation that recognizes care and respect for other cultures and ironic doubt about the claims of one's own culture. These obligations are sequential: recognition, respect, concern, care, and irony. An ethic of care is compatible with human rights and is logically necessary for the development of cultural rights. Care for the safety and security of other communities and cultures rests on our recognizing the precariousness of cultures in a global environment. An ironic distance from one's own culture remains a condition for recognizing the mutual vulnerability of humans.

REPRODUCTIVE AND SEXUAL RIGHTS

INTRODUCTION: PRECARIOUS SEX

We might reasonably argue that human beings are vulnerable precisely because they are sexual beings—that is, social beings whose sexual satisfaction and reproduction requires intimate reciprocity, typically with a limited number of partners over a considerable length of time. Humans cannot reproduce by cellular division, and they must seek out appropriate mates. Sexual acts, however fleeting and casual, require complex interactions with others. These encounters are typically institutionalized by various norms that attempt to regulate sexual activity, thereby reducing its complexity, uncertainty, and dangers. Despite these institutions, sexual encounters are inherently and irreducibly precarious. Sexual interaction invites us to pleasure and also exposes us to the possibilities of psychological embarrassment, social conflict, infection, and disease.

Reproductive and sexual rights are therefore closely associated with the general theme of vulnerability for at least four reasons. First, children, particularly unborn children, are the most vulnerable members of society. They are dependent on adults, especially parents and other kin, through much of their early development. They typically have no "voice" in community affairs, but they have to be closely nurtured and regulated because the continuity of the group or society depends on their successful training and socialization. Second, all sexual encounters open up opportunities for pleasure and mutuality but also for exploitation, oppression, and violence. We are easily wounded in sexual relations, often by people whom we love and trust. Relations between the sexes are therefore often combative and competitive, and, because women typically need to reproduce in order to acquire a status in the community, they are especially vulnerable. Third, in contemporary societies, where NRTs have expanded the range of choice for reproduction, medical technology increasingly influences reproductive rights. Medical technology's unintended consequences, though, often exacerbate the precariousness of social life. Finally, these reproductive rights straddle the distinction between individual human rights and the rights of citizens. The state has a crucial political interest in the reproduction of society and must develop, openly or covertly, eugenic strategies in order to safeguard its "breeding stock" and to maximize the advantages present in its own population.

In modern states, these reproductive choices are typically seen within a liberal ideology as aspects of private life. People are regarded as free to choose marriage partners and to reproduce under conditions that express their preferences. The reproductive rights of individuals are rarely exercised consciously as a contribution to state formation. Yet states constantly intervene into these reproductive strategies. For example, states organize tax regimes that influence people's preferences for childbearing, or encourage safe sex and contraception, or make certain sexual activities illegal by stipulating an appropriate age for consent to sex. The reproductive activities of adults are an important aspect of their lives as citizens, because states, through various means, normally reward heterosexual relations that reproduce society (typically through tax concessions and welfare benefits). In modern Japan and Singapore, for example, low birth rates have prompted both governments to encourage young couples to reproduce and take on the full duties of reproductive citizenship.

By contrast, human rights relating to reproduction have nothing to say explicitly about the social and political connections between nation building, state formation, and the role of the family, but these rights do relate very directly to patriarchal authority by claiming, for instance, that the selection of sexual partners should be voluntary. Human rights are also important when civil society has broken down and women and children are particularly exposed to the ravages of war and civil disorder through rape and other sexual violence.

The development of human rights protection for women especially emphasized protecting their reproductive rights as an aspect of their health care and their status in society. In societies where the state and civil society have broken down, new wars have made the position of women especially vulnerable. When the first Geneva Convention was signed in 1864, 90 percent of wartime casualties were soldiers; today over 90 percent are civilians, and women, increasingly, are the principal targets of violence. In May 2005, the Dutch Médecins Sans Frontières reported that five hundred women fleeing from local militia had been raped by Sudanese government soldiers. Such acts of violence have become commonplace in modern civil conflicts in failed states. There is also an important connection between famine, the HIV/AIDS epidemic, and new wars, all of which have had a devastating impact on the health and security of children. In these circumstances, traditional (that is, primarily religious) norms surrounding the conduct of family life and marriage have often been compromised by war and crime, and the precariousness of traditional institutions creates conditions for violent, radical social movements.

In traditional societies, religious institutions typically regulated sexual relations, marriage, and reproduction and provided some stability in social processes. The flow of resources (both material and cultural) from one generation to the next was organized by reference to a consensus about who could marry whom, when, and under what circumstances. Generally speaking, adults organized marriage contracts through arranged marriages within certain familial and kinship parameters. These arranged marriages were, of course, open to conflict and competition, but generally these processes could be arranged and evaluated by traditional norms. In modern societies, by comparison, marriage and divorce became increasingly open to individual choice, as adults claimed sexual rights to select their own marriage partners without overt interference from parents or kin. The existence of this open market does not mean that people are entirely free to select any sexual partner. Apart from rules relating to incest, legal norms govern age of consent, and there continues to be considerable social pressure toward heterosexual partnering. Modern societies have been characterized by considerable conflict over the status of gay and lesbian partnering or marriage as homosexual communities have appealed to a discourse of sexual rights to protect their right to choose sexual partners without public or legal constraint.

As a result, sexual rights have become very complex. With the development of secular citizenship through the nineteenth century as an aspect of nation building, reproduction became a fundamental duty of citizens who reproduced society by their own sexual reproduction. These citizens consequently claimed contributory rights in relation to the state. If adults take on the responsibility of reproducing children, then they can expect some level of support from the state (in terms of tax concessions, welfare benefits for children, or maternity and paternity leave), and in addition they may expect to receive some social status in the community as responsible parents. Gay and lesbian sexuality was historically a challenge to this conventional pattern of heterosexual reproduction. By definition, gay and lesbian sex does not result in biological reproduction, and hence these sexual orientations do not fit into a framework of social citizenship. The social rights of citizenship and the individual right of freedom to choose homosexual partners thus generate a certain tension. Conflict between these models produces proliferating concepts about different types of rights: sexual citizenship, intimate citizenship, reproductive rights, sexual rights, and rights for surrogacy, adoption, and so forth. One implicit governmental response to gay and lesbian rights has been to normalize these alternative sexual models around gay and lesbian marriage, or at least to encourage stability in such partnerships. Gay sexuality is not automatically seen to be deviant, insofar as gay men have, in many societies, access to normal roles through adoption, parenting, marriage, or some civil status. The traditional logic behind sexual activity in marriage was to reproduce and sustain society through heterosexual sex; gay and lesbian sexuality does not conform to this logic, but if alternative forms of partnering become available, then homosexual partnering comes to approximate the conventional model. A number of societies in Europe—among them Sweden, Spain, and Britain—have recognized civil marriage for same-sex couples.

The traditional model of social citizenship based on work, public service (such as military service), and reproduction is breaking down, because the traditional relationships between family, work, and marriage no longer hold. With the casualization of work and the changing nature of the workplace, the masculine role of father as sole breadwinner and the role of mother as domestic caregiver have become somewhat obsolete. Men, particularly poorly educated or unskilled workers, find it difficult to acquire sufficient continuity of work for them to enter careers that allow them to invest in family life, buy housing, and save for the future. They are also faced with competition from women: in the blue-collar strata, many women are better educated and more skilled than men. Technological change and competition have reduced the demand for labor in the advanced economies to such an extent that sociologists now talk about the problems of "capitalism without work" (Beck 2000). Supporting families over a life cycle in a post-Fordist economy has become difficult for men. There is a resultant general crisis in male identities in late capitalism—but the identities of women are also changing rapidly.

Traditional patterns of patriarchy within the family are being replaced by domestic situations that are more open to negotiation, and hence to conflict and competition. These tensions within the family are articulated as debates over the rights of its constituent members in terms of the rights of the child, women's rights, and (more recently) the rights of fathers to have equal access to children after divorce. In modern societies, these reproductive institutions have become precarious, and the uncertainties of daily life are expressed through conflicting discourses of rights. In short, modern liberal democracies are "risk societies" in which the conditions of successful partnering and reproduction are fragile and uncertain. In a risk environment, many communities turn to religion to shore up failing institutions; where necessary, they invent religious traditions to protect traditional norms regulating sexual behavior between men and women. Many aspects of rights abuse in sexual relationships emerge from the friction between traditional religious norms of sexual behavior and new circumstances in the sexual division of labor in the marketplace.

RELIGION, PATRIARCHY, AND REPRODUCTION

In order to understand the acrimonious debate around sexual rights, we need to understand the patriarchal nature of religion and its theological description of women's physical and spiritual vulnerability. The transformation of sexual relations and the growth of sexual rights have been vociferously (and occasionally violently) opposed by conservative religious groups, which typically claim that women are physically and psychologically vulnerable, thus requiring male protection. The Old Testament portrays female sexuality as dangerous and unpredictable, something to be regulated in the interest of the community. This myth, which is an important component of the Abrahamic religions of Judaism, Christianity, and Islam, serves to illustrate the importance of family and reproduction in sacred cosmologies. Divinity was, first and foremost, conceptualized as Fatherhood. Because these religious systems were (and continue to be) patriarchal, the contemporary transformations of family life, sexuality, the sexual division of labor, and the status of women have had profound and largely corrosive consequences for orthodox theology and religious practice.

The gospels do not contain a detailed, systematic view of sexual relations, marriage, and the family. In order to uncover the teaching of the early Church on marriage and family life, we have to turn to the letters of Saint Paul. The Pauline epistles, such as the letter to the Corinthians, were essentially *ad hoc* responses to specific local issues, but they have attained an enduring authority. Pauline theology precluded divorce; separated couples were not permitted to remarry. Celibacy was regarded as superior to marriage. Because the early Christian community was a millenarian movement, little was said about procreation. Later, when Christian theologians gave special attention to Mary's religious status, motherhood and child care gained significant recognition. In theological terms, Mary's virginity was necessary in order for Christ to be without sin, but Christ also had to be of woman born in order to be human and thus to experience our world. Over time, Mary herself was removed from the possibility of any connection with sin and became dissociated from the fall of Adam and Eve. The Catholic Church declared the doctrine of the Immaculate Conception in 1854, exempting Mary from original sin.

The women's movement, campaigns for gay and lesbian rights, and new medical technologies have significant implications for traditional religious cosmologies, but these social changes are themselves aspects of more general transformations in religious worldviews resulting from globalization. (These disruptions are not just consequential for Islamic orthodoxy or Muslim societies, as the recent crisis in the Anglican community over the ordination of a gay bishop in the American Episcopal Church demonstrates.) And these changing values around sexuality are, in many respects, themselves insignificant by comparison with the challenge from medical science. NRTS have, apart from anything else, severed the connection between sexual intercourse and reproduction. One immediate consequence of this technical development is that women have greater freedom to reproduce without the immediate intervention or interference of men. Reproduction for lesbian women is less socially problematic, for instance. These consequences are relatively well known and have been much celebrated by lesbian feminists.

There are, however, other possibilities. In the future, gay men might reproduce by the use of "artificial wombs," for example. In addition, age is now less significant in reproductive outcomes. With assisted reproduction, women over the age of sixty can give birth without apparent complication. We should avoid exaggerating the specific consequences of these reproductive opportunities, because the majority of married couples will continue to reproduce through sexual coitus, as previous generations have done. Still, the point is that these technical developments undermine the ideological authority of the conventional view of marriage, sex, and reproduction. Abortion on demand, surrogacy, same-sex marriage, lesbian parenting, gay fathers, no-fault divorce, gay bishops, test-tube babies, designer babies, and therapeutic cloning manifest a major revolution in sexuality, reproduction, and parenthood. These changes are not confined to Western liberal democracies.

In part, these developments in sexual rights are simply aspects of consumer culture: they illustrate the great range of choices that are open to individuals in shaping their reproductive careers. The consumer ethic proclaims that just as I am free to choose commodities, so I am free to choose my lifestyle. In fact, lifestyle *is* a commodity— possibly *the* commodity. I have rights as a consumer of commercial products. For example, through criminal law proceedings, I may be able to sue a company that sells me a car with defective tires that cause an injurious accident. In the same way, I have rights as a sexual being, because I can choose my partners without reference to rigid custom or tradition. In addition, if my partner has HIV but does not declare this condition and knowingly infects me, I may be able to bring a criminal case against him or her. It may also be advisable for the affluent elite to take out contracts before marriage to protect their assets in the event of divorce. This new market in sexual identities and practices creates new types of vulnerability, and in general, consumerism has influenced the erosion of marriage and family life. High divorce rates, serial monogamy, lone-parent families, and the isolation of men (and women) in later life can be taken as measures of the precariousness of modern familial institutions. Attempts to develop a code of rights for children, single mothers, or excluded fathers can be regarded as attempts to use rights as institutions to stabilize this competitive sexual marketplace.

SEXUAL RIGHTS AND PANDEMICS

The language of sexual rights is a language of advanced consumer societies. What, then, of sexual rights, reproduction, and health in so-called developing Third World societies? The situation of the Third World is clearly more desperate—and the notions of vulnerability and precariousness more pertinent. Women's health has been historically compromised by war, famine, and poverty, but with globalization, there are additional risks from the spread of new infections, especially

HIV/AIDS. Different manifestations of the AIDS epidemic reflect different social and political circumstances. In the industrial countries of the West, HIV/AIDS was originally spread through the affluent middle-class gay community. Public education, community politics, and drug therapy have contained this epidemic somewhat, and advanced care of HIV-infected people has extended their life expectancy. HIV/AIDS is also now prevalent among the heterosexual community, where safe-sex campaigns have been only partially effective. It is also a function of "poor etiquette" among drug-dependent populations. In three consecutive years (1996–98), the incidence of new AIDS cases decreased in western Europe, but they rose sharply in 2001–2.

Because AIDS is a condition that reflects changing patterns of human behavior, it is spreading rapidly in socially deprived groups in eastern Europe. In Africa and Asia, where 95 percent of the world's HIV population is located, it has been primarily a condition of the heterosexual majority community and is thus widespread among children. In sub-Saharan Africa, there are just under thirty million people infected with HIV/AIDS. Fifteen million have died from AIDS. Three and a half million were infected in 2002, but only a small minority is receiving any antiretroviral therapy. This epidemic often combines with existing poverty, low education, civil strife and warfare, and environmental catastrophe. A third of people in Botswana aged 15 to 49 are HIV positive, and there are thirteen million AIDS orphans in Africa as a whole. The drugs that can delay HIV's developing into AIDS are beyond the reach of many poor countries. The Centre for the Protection of Children's Rights estimates that in Thailand, with a population of sixty million, there are around three million prostitutes—of whom almost a third are children. HIV/AIDS is spreading quickly, primarily through girls. It has also spread rapidly in Russia, eastern Europe, and China, where one can argue that social disruption, rapid urbanization, and industrialization have produced an AIDS epidemic, especially where governments have refused to recognize its existence. The AIDS outbreak in Russia is associated with the deterioration of the social fabric following the disruptions of the old Soviet system and the rise of a market economy. AIDS increases match the rapid rises in crime, alcoholism, and drug abuse. AIDS raises crucial gender questions, too, as poverty in contemporary Russia has often forced women into prostitution to support their families. In Russian seaports, the spread of HIV among sex workers and injecting drug users (IDUS) plays an important bridging role to the rest of the population. In China, AIDS is common in economically marginal regions where people have been exposed to contaminated blood. China's government has been slow to recognize or take measures against AIDS. It now recognizes almost a million cases, but this is certainly an underestimate.

The vulnerable status of women and children is historically associated with the impact of infectious disease, warfare, and poverty, but globalization has exacerbated this vulnerability. Again, the concept of new wars is useful for thinking about women's increased vulnerability. In conventional inter-state wars that involved large set battles and military maneuvers, sexual violence against women on enemy territory was dysfunctional in terms of military rationality. It interfered with the primary objective of war: the defeat of an opposing army by direct military engagement. Harassing local populations constrained military mobility on the battlefield and delayed engagement with the enemy. The development of international law to protect civilians was perfectly compatible with the military objectives of such conventional wars. In new wars, this logic evaporates. The rape of women and overall violence toward civilians become functional activities in undermining judicial institutions, civil authorities, and civil society. In old wars between states, the majority of casualties were military personnel; in new wars, the casualties are almost entirely civilian. The male body was the target of old wars, but the rape and killing of the female body are central to new wars. Rape signifies to local communities that their men have been defeated, that they cannot protect their own women. In symbolic terms, they are no longer men. Violence against women appears to be most prevalent in societies that have had strict sexual and moral codes, and mass rape thus signifies the collapse of the existing regime. The rape of women in Bangladesh by Pakistani soldiers in the war of 1971, of Hazara women around Mazar-i-Sharif by Taliban forces, of Algerian women by armed groups associated with the Islamic Salvation Front, of Bosnian women by Serbian Chetniks, or of East Timorian women by Indonesian men is evidence of "the extensive sexualization of violence that is observable in nearly all the new wars. . . . War here becomes one big torture machine whose purpose is to produce pain and suffering [rather than] to enforce a political will" (Münkler 2005, 86). Such sexualized violence destroys its victims in terms of their symbolic value as human beings within a functioning community, and it further dehumanizes the perpetrators, because they can no longer recognize or admit a shared vulnerability.

REPRODUCTIVE, SEXUAL, AND INTIMATE RIGHTS

In recent years, there has been a growing concern to expand the concept of citizenship to embrace the rights of sexual citizenship (Bell and Binnie 2000; Richardson and Seidman 2002). In addition, there is the notion of "intimate citizenship," expressing certain rights to intimate relations with people of one's own choice, including people of one's own sex. We also need to consider the notion of "reproductive rights" and define these rights accurately. A reproductive right is the right to choose one's sexual partner, without undue restraint, with the intention of having a child whose own chances of survival are not compromised. Reproductive rights are associated with the notion that reproduction is an aspect of healthy living and that involuntary infertility is damaging to the partners' mental health. A sexual right may be initially defined as the right to select one's sexual partner without external (state) interference. A sexual right need not entail any desire to reproduce, because the issue is more concerned with freedom to select partners. These rights are designed to protect gay and lesbian partnerships in which there is no necessary intention to form a family. Further still, one might identify a right to sexual pleasure or "intimate citizenship" in which it is claimed that there is a right to sexual activity (in private) that should not necessarily be the concern of the state. I shall now consider these claims in more detail.

Reproductive rights are enshrined in Article 16 of the Universal Declaration of Human Rights, which recognizes that men and women "have a right to marry and to found a family" and that "marriage shall be entered into only with the free and full consent of the intending spouses." We might also assume that this reproductive right is associated with Article 3 ("everyone has the right to life"), which we might extend to the idea that everyone has a right to make life. These human rights clearly indicate that forced marriage is an infringement and that, in certain circumstances, arranged marriage might be incompatible with the spirit of Article 16. These rights within the Declaration have nothing to say about duties, but we might reasonably assume that the duty that corresponds to a right to reproduce is a duty to protect one's offspring and to ensure that a child's health is not compromised by the parents' lifestyle. For example, excessive tobacco or alcohol use by the parents might be regarded as a failure of parental duty toward an unborn child. Reproductive rights are, however, primarily about the exercise of free choice in the selection of partners and about personal autonomy in the conditions under which reproduction takes place. Obviously, medical science becomes very important in the exercise of this right by maximizing the opportunities for reproduction.

Reproductive rights can be understood as aspects of the capabilities model (Nussbaum 2000). Nussbaum's list of "central human functional capabilities" includes "bodily health," which she describes as "being able to have good health, including reproductive health." Economic development cannot take place without the development of social and political rights, and social development cannot take place without women's equality, especially through the provision of education. Women's social rights are very closely connected with their reproductive rights. Article 12 of the Convention on the Elimination of Discrimination Against Women (1997) says that states should "take all appropriate measures to eliminate discrimination against women in the field of health care in order to ensure, on a basis of equality with men and women, access to health care services, including those relating to family planning."

The 1994 International Conference on Population and Development recognized the importance of a satisfying and safe sexual life as the basis of the capability to reproduce and the freedom to choose when and how to reproduce. Reproductive citizenship can also be said to include a right *not* to reproduce. Human rights conventions include the protection of women (and men) from the threat of rape, especially sexual violence and collective slavery in war conditions. Clearly illustrating the recognition of such rights, the Hague tribunal on Yugoslav war crimes decided to regard the rape of Muslim women during the Bosnia crisis of 1992–95 as a crime against humanity. The tribunal elevated mass rape from a mere violation of the "customs of war" to a heinous crime. By contrast, sexual citizenship promotes the idea of sexual intimacy as a right and makes no assumptions about reproduction. It is more concerned to promote the idea of freedom of sexual expression and association, and sexual rights thus aim to establish the conditions of sexual difference and recognition.

Reproductive rights pose some interesting problems, however. They have to pay some attention to the issue of what we might call "the best product," namely, healthy children. It is in the interest of parents to have "high quality" offspring (in genetic terms), and they may also want to limit the number of their offspring to enhance their children's life chances over time. Parents therefore might want easy and regular recourse to contraception and possibly abortion in order to manage the number of children they have. Aborting pregnancies where it is known that the child is, from a medical point of view, unlikely to be healthy is consistent with exercising parental responsibility to have the best outcome. Are there different reproductive rights and possibly conflicting interests between parents and children? Reproductive rights (such as the right to reproduce under conditions of one's own choosing) primarily involve the rights and duties of parenting, not necessarily the rights of an unborn child. The legislation relating to reproductive citizenship attempts to provide a legal answer to the question of with whom, and under what social and legal conditions, one may reproduce. By contrast, sexual citizenship concerns the rights of sexual consumption—that is, with whom one may enjoy sexual intimacy, what forms of intimacy are legitimate, and under what conditions one may find sexual fulfillment.

Is there a natural right to reproduce? Is there a right to reproduce regardless of age? In the United Kingdom, Liz Buttle, a 60-year-old Welsh hill farmer who received medical support for assisted reproduction, became the oldest mother in Britain in 1997 after lying about her age to the medical authorities. In 2000, a couple aged 55 and 56 had twins following treatment for reproductive assistance. A British woman aged 58 is currently (in 2005) to become a mother following egg donation at a private clinic. The argument against treatment of women over 50 years (women experiencing or completing menopause) is mainly that the physical demands of labor will probably produce complications, such as high blood pressure. Such medical arguments appear to ignore completely social arguments about the responsibilities of parenting. In the 1990s, the average life expectancy for women in the United Kingdom was 79 years; for men, it was 74. A woman giving birth at 60 would in all probability still be alive by the time her offspring had reached maturity at nineteen years of age. The husband might still be alive by the time the child was fourteen years. We might assume, however, that if both parents were retired at 65 years of age, they would have difficulty supporting a child through its schooling.

These examples of assisted reproduction raise serious questions about whether reproduction in old age is socially responsible. What we might describe as "geriatric reproduction" is certainly feasible with new technologies, but is it socially and psychologically desirable? Can the parents (or parent) make an adequate contribution to the mental and physical well-being of the child? With stem-cell research, it may be possible to increase life expectancy, and if female life expectancy were to increase by a decade in the near future, with new technologies women might be able to reproduce in their seventies or eighties. From an economic point of view, it would appear that these "geriatric parents" could not easily or adequately support their children into maturity. With gamete donation and modern techniques for the storage of human tissue, it is possible to reproduce from parents who are already dead. These medical possibilities raise questions about the justice of reproductive circumstances. Young couples, for example, who may be alcoholic, unemployed, and have criminal records are not prevented by the law courts from exercising their right to reproduce. Should we prevent responsible and respectable couples in mid- to late life from having access to reproductive technologies in order to have children?

Still, these arguments are not wholly convincing, because they raise a question about how parents in general might ensure the "best product." There is a eugenics argument that parents who have a serious genetically transferable condition should not have children—and even that parents who happen to have less serious diseases, such as diabetes, should not reproduce, because there is a high chance that their children will also be diabetic. Medical technology has made it possible for parents to have "designer babies," but in practice, these are rare, and the implication of the metaphor of design can be misleading. "Designing" babies in practice means counseling for inherited, rare conditions. For example, the Human Fertilisation and Embryology Act in Great Britain supported two cases where parents had conceived children in order to provide an existing infant with genetic therapy in order to seek a cure for leukemia and thalassemia. In the United States, the deliberate decision of Sharon Duchesneau and Candy McCullough, a deaf lesbian couple, to have a deaf baby has been controversial. The implication of these examples is that medical science expands the possibilities for people to exercise their right to reproduce, but at the same time it makes these choices more complex and uncertain. The social applications of medical science often increase the precariousness of social institutions (in this case, familial institutions) and at the same time, in many circumstances, they reduce the vulnerability of both parents and children.

These issues bring out an essential aspect of reproductive rights: unlike sexual rights, they necessarily entail the rights of others, especially offspring. They therefore illustrate the crucial matter of obligation in any discussion of rights. If we grant full and effective reproductive rights to women (or, more generally, to parents), do children have comparable rights? Children depend on advocacy if they are to realize their rights effectively, and the obvious problem is that children generally cannot exercise their rights without the full backing and assistance of their parents. Yet parental rights (to selection, contraception, abortion, and divorce) may not always coincide with children's rights. In fact, children's rights may very frequently conflict with parental rights.

HUMAN RIGHTS, WOMEN, AND NEW WARS

There are clearly major differences between gay and lesbian move-ments in the Western world claiming equal sexual rights and the plight of women in parts of India who are forced to sell kidneys to provide money to support their families. Equally, there is an evident contrast in terms of choice between middle-class professional women delaying reproduction in the Western world in order to sustain a ca-reer and the reproductive history of Muslim women in Bangladesh. Despite these obvious contrasts between the developed and the devel-oping world, there is at least one connecting thread here: the radical transformation of men's economic status in global capitalism. Global-ization and the transformation of the world economy from the 1970s on have had contradictory consequences that partly explain the associ-ation between the social marginalization of men, the rise of religious and political radicalism, and violence.

The worldwide decline in family size—that is, in female fertility in marriage—has played an important part in liberating women, allow-ing them to participate more actively in economic roles in the formal labor market and in political roles within civil society. While declining family size is often seen as a consequence of modernization, the argu-ment can easily be reversed to say that the control of female fertility allowed women to become modern by freeing them from more or less lifelong careers in pregnancy. Yet these democratic and economic improvements for women have often occurred alongside declining op-portunities for men. Social violence, therefore, has an important gen-der dimension, and these demographic changes are partly expressed in sexual violence in new wars.

With economic modernization and globalization, economic roles for men in labor-intensive activities have been disappearing. By con-trast, service industries and non-manual activities have given women new economic opportunities (in communications, for example). In so-cieties with very high unemployment, young men in particular find themselves unemployed or underemployed, and their economic mar-ginalization means that they cannot enter easily into marriage and family building. Their economic inactivity robs them of social status.

Meanwhile, the world entertainment industry, which is primarily American, feeds them with images of masculinity based on pure violence. Sylvester Stallone, Bruce Willis, Arnold Schwarzenegger, and Clint Eastwood offer young men alternative role models in which social and hence sexual power comes out of the barrel of a gun. In short, the loss of economic power is compensated through the acquisition, either in fantasy or reality, of a warrior role in the social organization of violence. Indeed, we could express this transition within a Marxist terminology: men who have been ejected from the economic mode of production, where they increasingly constitute a surplus population, can find new roles in a mode of violence, in which they can be fully employed.

Violent religious and political movements or cults, such as Hamas, Sikh militancy, Shining Path, and Aum Shinrikyo, can be seen as the social consequences of psychological frustrations—frustrations following from global neoliberal changes that gained momentum in the 1970s and stimulated economic crises (Juergensmeyer 2000). The demographic revolution of the twentieth century produced large cohorts of young men, who, while often well educated to college or university level, could not find employment opportunities to satisfy aspirations inflamed by nationalist governments and ideologies.

In political terms, Palestine has been the single most important issue nurturing global political Islam, but in more general sociological terms, twentieth-century Islamic jihadism arose from the frustrations of those social strata (civil servants, teachers, engineers, technicians, and college lecturers) whose interests had not been adequately served by either the secular nationalism of Gamal Abdel Nasser, Muhammad Reza Shah Pahlavi, Suharto, or Saddam Hussein or the neoliberal strategies of Anwar Sadat in Egypt or Chadli Benjedid in Algeria. The social and economic dislocations created by global economic reform produced ideal conditions for external Western support of those secular elites in the Arab world and elsewhere who would benefit significantly from oil revenues. These changes, then, created states that were dependent on oil revenues, which in turn promoted authoritarianism. In short, jihadism is a product of a religious crisis of authority, the failures of nationalist governments, and the socioeconomic divisions exacerbated by neoliberal economic globalization.

The linkages between social frustration, failed expectations, and radical religious movements have been confirmed by sociological research (Roy 2004) that demonstrates that political Islam and the jihadists are not a special case. Rather, there are common social and psychological threads to religious violence across the globe. These include antipathy to the emancipation of women and the assertion of women's rights, hatred and fear of homosexuality, and support for the restoration of polygamous marriage. These themes exist in radical politicized religions because the men who are attracted to them see the presence of gay men and liberated women as symbols of their own powerlessness and loss of social status. In North America, figures such as Timothy McVeigh, the Oklahoma City bomber, represent the aggression and frustration of straight men (many of whom have served in the military) with liberal society, in which sexual rights have significantly expanded. Fundamentalism, violent politics, and aggression are associated with these experiences of powerlessness and humiliation among young, marginalized men. Political sacrifice, as illustrated by suicide bombings, provides a solution to this worldly psychic deprivation, especially when sacrificial death provides what Juergensmeyer has called "symbolic empowerment."

Perhaps the plight and desperation of young men in Palestinian refugee camps is the most tragic illustration of this theme in the Middle East. Honor killings have greatly increased in the occupied territories, secular Palestinian women more frequently adopt the veil, and evidence collected by Palestinian social workers and psychologists indicate a sharp rise in sexual abuse and domestic violence cases. Social reports from the occupied territories show that family life has been profoundly disrupted in refugee camps, and traditional patterns of courtship, marriage, and family life are difficult to sustain. Men in detention or prison can no longer exercise long-established authority over their families, especially their daughters. High levels of unemployment have undermined the sense of self-worth and privilege traditionally enjoyed by men. Finally, the curfews imposed on towns and camps by the Israeli military mean that normal patterns of sociability are undermined; in particular, young men are confined to the home, with television their only source of leisure and entertainment. Domestic spaces become sites of psychological tension and physical violence. The victimization of women is reduced by veiling, because the women can emphasize both their opposition to Israeli occupation and their loyalty to Palestinian culture. The veil protects them from Israeli men and expresses their conformity to the Palestinian family. The overrepresentation of women among suicide bombers in conflicts against Israeli civilian targets reflects this pressure on women, who are thought to have lost their honor and who seek collective redemption through self-sacrifice.

CONCLUSION: RIGHTS AND THE CRISIS OF MODERN SEXUALITY

Palestine may be the extreme case, but these social conflicts are also present in Afghanistan, Iraq, Chechnya, and Cambodia, where massive social disruption undermines the traditional authority of men and produces a collective paranoia about the sexual virtue of women. There appears to be a relationship between the erosion of male (patriarchal) authority, the repression of women, political violence, and religious revival. The Taliban are one example, but hostility to sexual rights for gays, pro-life values, and attempts to domesticate female labor are common among all fundamentalist groups. A similar mixture of powerlessness, economic unemployment, and anti-Semitism fueled fascist ideology, militaristic youth movements, hostility toward assertive women, and hatred of homosexuality in the interwar period in Germany (Theweleit 1987).

A distinction can be drawn between traditional patriarchy, which has the force of law and religious sanction, and "patrism," which operates in deregulated and uncertain social spaces between men and women (Turner 1984). While traditional and formal patterns of patriarchy as prescribed by religious systems of power clearly subordinated and regulated women, gender conflict may be paradoxically greater in patrism, with formal power over women removed or eroded. The disruptions of globalization may further intensify gender conflict, as men perhaps attempt to restore the traditional legitimacy of patriarchal authority (with an appeal to religion as a sanction of male power and female submission). With patrism, the rules surrounding sexual relationships become unclear and thus open to more negotiation, misunderstanding, and conflict. Gay and lesbian sexualities appear to flaunt the customary values of male power and an apparently "natural," religiously supported sexual division of labor. Patrism offers us a concept that explains how sexual relationships and practices become uncertain and precarious with social change. The decline in female fertility is the collective expression of new reproductive and sexual rights, but the resistance of traditionalists and fundamentalists to women's changing status constitutes an important dimension of modern social conflict.

RIGHTS OF IMPAIRMENT AND DISABILITY

INTRODUCTION: WELFARE CITIZENSHIP

Citizenship and social rights have passed through several stages in modern social and political thought—from the idealism of the philosopher T. H. Green before the First World War to the development of European welfare policies after the Second World War, policies that were associated with social Keynesianism and specifically with T. H. Marshall, Richard Titmuss, J. M. Keynes, and William Beveridge. The modern debate about citizenship has concentrated on Marshall's *Citizenship and Social Class and Other Essays* (1950). In the United States, Talcott Parsons and Kenneth Clark in *The American Negro* (1966) and Reinhard Bendix in *Nation-Building and Citizenship* (1964) took up Marshall's ideas in mainstream sociology. Contemporary interest in citizenship theory is the product of a variety of changing circumstances: the problems of European integration, the transformation of the welfare state, the politics of gay liberation, social movements to protect the environment, the conflict between aboriginal rights and national governments, the persistence of economic inequality along ethnic and gender lines, and, finally, the challenge of new medical technologies to traditional relationships (namely, parenting, household formation, work, and the state). These substantive topics all raise the question of the relationships among sovereign states, social citizenship, and human rights.

Citizenship rights have been extensively debated with respect to ethnicity, gender, and class, but the issue of the rights of people with impairments decisively illustrates the differences between citizenship and human rights. Conventional forms of citizenship were associated with the modernization of society, nation building, and the development of modern states' administrative framework. The national structure of citizenship was assumed to have universal relevance. Ethnic diversity, multiculturalism, and the globalization of cultures have challenged the traditional assumptions of a common process of modernization. At the same time, contemporary acceptance of anthropological relativism, with its emphasis on cultural diversity and difference, has made universal standards of justice and equality problematic.

The modern period—specifically since the late 1960s—has been characterized by the erosion of the Marshallian model of citizenship. The current crises of citizenship and multiculturalism open up the possibility of post-national patterns of membership, but they also raise difficult questions about political authority, identity, and responsibility. The transformation of the national framework of social rights suggests that entitlements, especially for marginal and subordinated social groups, are perhaps more appropriately couched in the language of human rights rather than the language of national citizenship. In this respect, Francis Fukuyama (2002, 108) is surely correct in saying that "the language of rights has become, in the modern world, the only shared and widely intelligible vocabulary we have for talking about ultimate goods or ends, and in particular those collective goods or ends that are the stuff of politics." The only question is this: What kind of rights? My argument is that the language of human rights is ultimately the only plausible language for expressing the needs of people with impairment and disability, that is, for social groups that fall outside the Marshallian model of citizenship and welfare that dominated postwar social policy.

A MODEL OF SOCIAL CITIZENSHIP

Citizenship can be divided into three aspects: civil, political, and social. The civil dimension of citizenship was necessary for the achievement of individual freedoms, and it included such features as freedom of speech, the right to own property, and the right to justice. The political element comprised the rights to participate in the exercise of political power (such as the right to free elections), to join political parties, and to have a secret ballot. Finally, the social component is the right to "a modicum of economic welfare and security to the right to share to the full in the social heritage and to live the life of a civilized being" (Marshall 1950, 69). These three dimensions evolved from the seventeenth century to the twentieth and became established through a process of institutional differentiation, as special agencies developed to express these rights. Alongside these three components, a set of institutions gives these rights concrete social expression: namely, the courts of justice, parliament, political parties and councils of local government, the educational system, and welfare services.

In principle, citizenship modifies the negative impact of the capitalist market through a redistribution of resources on the basis of social rights. Hence there is a permanent tension between the principles of equality and justice that underpin liberal democracy and the actual inequalities of wealth and power that characterize the capitalist economy. The contradiction between inherited wealth and the norms of fairness is particularly problematic in societies that promote individual achievement, social mobility, and equality, but inherited personal wealth has proved difficult to change through taxation, partly because inherited resources are important for family continuity. Within liberal democracy, there is thus a dynamic and contradictory relationship between capitalism and citizenship—or, in more general terms, between scarcity and solidarity. In the postwar period, Marshallian citizenship in Britain and elsewhere came to institutionalize the ideals and aspirations of social and economic reconstruction (that was in turn an expression of Keynesianism). In this sense, citizenship is a status position that mitigates or modifies the negative effects of economic and social inequality within capitalist society.

Marshall's analysis of citizenship rights has been critically attacked on several grounds. It failed to identify a definite causal mechanism to explain the historical growth of citizenship. British sociology has characteristically argued that the growth of social rights in the nineteenth and twentieth centuries emerged from working-class conflicts over economic rights relating to employment, fair dismissal, unionization, sickness benefit, and retirement. Yet there are obviously important historical differences between the American and British experiences. In Britain, the main irritant behind the growth of social rights has been class inequality in relation to fundamental resources such as housing, health care, education, and social security. By contrast, American citizenship has been largely inspired by the issues of slavery, ethnicity, migration, and social mobility. The American experience of citizenship has revolved around the success and failure of civic ideals in a context of slavery, racial division, and ethnic conflict. A more critical view suggests that individual rights in the United States—that is, negative liberties—have always been precariously secured and that, given a history of slavery, American political culture has been a "liberalism of fear" (Shklar 1998, 116).

The other major causal feature in the development of citizenship in both America and Britain has been the unintended consequence of modern warfare. Although the idea of a comprehensive health system had been much discussed in Britain before the First World War, it gained widespread acceptance during the Second World War, and the Labour Government of Prime Minister Clement Attlee (1945–51) created a national health service offering free treatment to all citizens. The welfare state in Britain after the Second World War and the civil rights movement in America after the Vietnam War both responded to the mass mobilization of society and to its self-critical reflection. Richard Titmuss drew attention (1962) to the unintended consequences of warfare on social reform by noting that war induces societies to undertake a self-critical appraisal of their values and institutions. There may be an important difference, however, in terms of the impact of old wars on social citizenship and new wars on human rights in the historical growth of such juridical concepts of entitlement and security. If mass warfare contributed to the growth of welfare rights, then new wars have been a catalyst for contemporary human rights legislation and intervention.

Marshall's view of citizenship also presupposed a more or less homogenous society in which cultural, religious, and ethnic divisions were less important than the divisions of social class. The social context of British citizenship had been described in uncompromising terms by George Orwell in *The Road to Wigan Pier* in 1937. Orwell's shattering description of the economic and cultural divisions in British society had an important shock value for the middle classes, who were largely unaware of working-class deprivation. British welfare reform was intended to provide a remedy for such degrading social and cultural conditions. Not surprisingly, then, social rights reform largely aimed to modify social class inequalities.

Marshall's theory also assumed a neat relationship between right and duty. Effective entitlement has depended, in practice, on three contributions: work, war, and parenting. In historical terms, social citizenship has been closely associated with the involvement of individuals (typically men) in the formal labor market. Work was fundamental to the conception of the citizen in all forms of the welfare state. Individuals could achieve effective entitlements through the production of goods and services (that is, through gainful employment), which was essential for investment in adequate pensions and superannuation after retirement. These entitlements also typically included insurance coverage (against accidents, illness, and short-term unemployment), health care, and retirement benefits. The idea that the citizen has a basic duty of work is fundamental to civic society, as clearly recognized in John Locke's political theory.

If we regard employment as *de facto* a fundamental condition of social participation, then physical impairment often prevents people from participating as effective citizens. The underlying assumptions are that there is a necessary conceptual connection between a right and a duty and, empirically, an almost perfect balance between entitlements and contributions. These assumptions are controversial, because in practice there is no neat correlation between right and duty. For example, in ethical discourse we often ascribe a moral status to the human embryo and hence attribute rights to unborn children. Prolife activists believe that abortion is murder, a denial of the rights of the fetus. While children may have rights, it is not clear that they have duties, and there are thus many circumstances in which there does not appear to be a clear empirical connection between rights and duties.

Moreover, military service to the state through warfare creates entitlements for soldier-citizens. Military service often results in special pension rights, health provisions, housing, and education for returning servicemen and servicewomen and their families. In Australia, for example, the interests of ex-servicemen were expressed through the Return Serviceman's League, a powerful lobby group that has secured benefits for its members. In America, returning servicemen, especially black Americans, created a powerful lobby for the reform of civil liberties. One can anticipate a similar development after servicemen and servicewomen return from duty in Iraq, and there is already considerable discussion of the claims that military personnel will make on the state as a result of post-traumatic illness. War service has been crucial, therefore, in the evolution of social security entitlements.

In addition, young couples achieve entitlements by forming households and families that become the social mechanisms for the reproduction of society through the birth, socialization, and education of children. With increasing longevity and decline in family size, these services also include care for the aging and elderly, as generational obligations are satisfied through the domestic sphere. These services to the state through the family and household provide entitlements to both men and women as parents—as reproducers of the nation. These parental entitlements become the basis of family security systems, various types of support for mothers, and health and educational provisions for infants and children.

The intimate sexual activity of adults in marriage is regarded in law as a private matter, but the state and church have historically taken an enduring interest in the moral conditions for lawful union and for the reproductive consequences of lawful (and unlawful) sexual activity. Sustaining and legitimating heterosexual reproduction has been a major objective of the regulatory activity of the modern state: the values and norms of a household constituted by a married heterosexual couple provide the dominant ideal of social life in modern society, despite the fact that four in ten live births in Britain in the late 1990s, for example, occurred outside wedlock, and that 30 percent of one-family households had no children. The moral force of the idea of marriage and domesticity is so compelling in contemporary society that many states have sought to permit gay couples to form civil unions that would give them the rights and benefits currently legally available to married heterosexual couples. While legislation was introduced into the British parliament in 2004 to make civil partnership a legally recognized relationship, the main problem in British common law historically has centered on how to define "a couple" in a manner that is legally secure. There has been no such traditional status as a "common-law wife." The issue has not been simply about homosexual unions, then, but about the legal status of any long-standing mutual union outside of a legal marriage.

These three conditions of effective entitlement create a pattern of active participation in society that, in turn, supports civil society through the production of social capital. Citizens' active participation in the labor market also maintains work-related associations such as workingmen's clubs, trade union organizations and guilds, and political organizations. These organizations are, in fact, "intermediary associations" (Durkheim 1992)—that is, associations that occupy the space between the state and the individual, provide moral regulation of society, and mediate between the individual and the state. These heterogeneous community associations—football clubs, chapels, fan clubs, gardening clubs, women's circles, and ethnic associations— have been identified as an essential aspect of communal cohesiveness. In general, warfare in the twentieth century has been destructive of traditional patterns of civil association, but one unintended consequence of these military conflicts has been to produce a multitude of associations offering support and services to ex-soldiers. The ceremonials of male solidarity (military parades of veterans and other public rituals of remembrance) kept alive the intense comradeship of combat, and in the United Kingdom the famous "Dunkirk spirit" constituted the benchmark of national solidarity, civilian service, and individual sacrifice.

Again, citizen rights are contributory rights, and they correspond, more or less, to a set of duties typically expressed through work, war, and parenthood. There is no corresponding set of duties in the case of human rights. In addition, human rights institutions offer fewer opportunities for the creation of social capital and social cohesiveness. The social rights of citizens are couched in a civil society that mediates between state and society. There is, at present, no effective global human rights civil society, but there is a rapidly emerging network of international nongovernmental organizations that could potentially function as a global civil society, one capable of offsetting the negative consequences of economic individualism and healing the disruptive consequences of rapid global change. Anti-globalization movements are also connected to a multitude of local nongovernmental associations that create both local and global patterns of social solidarity.

CITIZENSHIP, DISABILITY, AND SOCIAL CONSTRUCTION

Contributory citizen rights are based on the principle of lifelong contributions to collective resources. They assume a close (if imprecise) relationship between rights and duties—that is, between entitlement and effort. People can, in principle, choose to increase their contributions in the anticipation of higher rewards in the future, and these investments allow people to draw retrospectively on their past contributions. It is assumed, therefore, that lifelong contributions correlate, over the long term, with benefits, and that there is some degree of fairness between effort and reward.

Unfortunately, these assumptions do not easily fit the life chances of the disabled, especially those who are disabled from birth. Because effective citizenship has been based on work, war, and reproduction, disability has typically limited the enjoyment of such entitlements. Those with disability are often excluded from full-time employment; they cannot be active members of the armed forces; and they are, often for medical reasons, not able to reproduce. Because they do not fully satisfy the duties of the "able-bodied citizen," they do not have easy access to the full range of rights that are characteristic of citizens at work. As a result, "disability" is often described not as physical impairment, but as a loss of social rights (Barnes, Mercer, and Shakespeare 1999). The social rights of Marshallian citizenship have not always served disabled people adequately, and citizenship often appears to favor duties over rights in any case. Hence human rights discourse has an obvious appeal to the disability movement: human rights do not require a close or necessary connection between entitlements and contributions and are not inevitably connected with the narrow contributory model of national social citizenship (Bickenbach 2001).

While the social rights of national citizenship often collide with the individual rights of universal human rights legislation, the Declaration's individualistic tradition of civil and political rights has been increasingly influenced by the social dimension of the International Covenant on Economic, Social, and Cultural Rights. The national framework of disability organizations is also being replaced by international organizations, as the disability movement becomes a global social movement. The Disabled People's International (DPI), for example, was created in 1981 and held its first world congress in Singapore. The DPI exists as a political grassroots organization to advance debate on impairments and disability as consequences of war, inequality, poverty, and industrial exploitation. In the future, we can expect that the issues of disability and impairment will be addressed not by the framework of citizenship in nation-states, but by human rights in the framework of global governance. In part, the disabilities that result from modern warfare and civil conflict cannot be adequately addressed, let alone resolved, by nation-states, often because the scale of these social disasters cannot be managed by states alone. Disabilities arising from the use of antipersonnel mines in Africa or from conflicts in Central Asia and Afghanistan would be obvious examples. Similarly, the disabilities that will result from the tsunami in southeast Asia and the earthquake in northern Pakistan in 2005 cannot be addressed or managed by individual governments working independently.

The Marshallian model of the welfare state has also been criticized because it promoted bureaucratic welfare strategies that were insensitive to cultural differences, employing undemocratic and patronizing methods that normalized conditions that were deemed to be socially deviant. Managing mental abnormality and physical disability through "total institutions" was famously criticized by sociologists (Goffman

1961). Social inclusion often meant, in practice, the normalization and suppression of difference in the interest of social uniformity and social control. The medicalization of disability has often meant that social rights and individual needs could be ignored by treating the impairment rather than attending to the person. In response, alternative strategies of deinstitutionalization were adopted in the 1970s, but these strategies of "decarceration" were subsequently criticized when they were seen to be merely a cost-cutting management exercise. Successful deinstitutionalization requires significant professional and community support if it is to provide adequate alternative forms of care. These issues surrounding the framework of institutional care expose a more fundamental problem of social inclusion versus personal autonomy.

The tensions and contradictions between social rights, inclusion, and normalization can be illustrated by the history of the treatment of deafness, which provides us with an important example of the social and political issues that surround physical impairment. The social struggles over the rights of deaf people expose the contradictory processes of inclusion and exclusion that frequently attend disability and impairment. The traditional response to deafness, especially to prelingual deafness, was to treat it as a personal tragedy. Those who were unable to acquire speech were automatically labeled as "dumb" or "mute." Before the late eighteenth century, there was little prospect that people with hearing impairments could acquire any education, and their social opportunities for employment and marriage were severely limited. They were effectively segregated culturally from society and were treated as second-class citizens. Medical interest in the diseases of the ear had begun in seventeenth-century France, but the important advances were educational and cultural, not simply medical. Eventually, as a consequence of the civil rights movement and the political organization of the deaf themselves, social attitudes toward deaf people began to change in the late twentieth century.

The real problem is that while deafness is an impairment of hearing, it is readily transformed into a social disability, involving a denial of social rights and status. There is a Deaf culture and a Deaf community that include both people with a congenital hearing impairment and hearing people who, as the children of deaf people, grew up in the sign language community. Like other minority cultures, the Deaf community is held together culturally and socially by a separate and distinctive language and by the personal experiences of exclusion and stigmatization. In this example of deafness, we discover an important insight into the intersection between bodily impairment, the historical stigma of being a "deaf-mute," and the political mobilization of a community to achieve social citizenship. It also illustrates that social inclusion is often achieved at the cost of difference and distinctiveness. One challenge to the National Association of the Deaf as an ascriptive identity group has been the growing medical use of cochlear implants to provide deaf children with hearing. Because 90 percent of deaf children are born to hearing parents, the contemporary use of cochlear implants has the unintended consequence of undermining the distinctive existence of a special Deaf community.

THE BODY, RIGHTS, AND SOCIAL REALITY

These issues about deafness and hearing impairment raise more general questions about the nature and status of such conditions and ultimately about their ontology. The political articulation of the rights of disabled people has been associated with various sociological theories that claim that medical conditions can be regarded as socially constructed rather than natural phenomena. The social theory of Peter Berger and Thomas Luckmann (1967) on "the social construction of reality" facilitated the development of the disability movement, because this sociological theory of the social organization of knowledge provided an epistemological basis for what is known as the "social model of disability." The sociology of knowledge helped promote the view among activists that disability was socially constructed; rather than being a self-evident physical condition, disability was the pernicious outcome of social processes of classification and exclusion. This sociological perspective proved to be key in recasting the definition of disability as a denial of civil rights rather than simply a taken-for-granted natural impairment of the body. The vulnerability of the disabled is, according to this view, socially and politically produced.

There is now greater public awareness that the prejudicial assumptions of the media and the employment of a "disabling language" in society reinforce negative stereotypes of disability. The disability movement claims that there is an ideology of "ableism" that functions to exclude people who do not conform to a conventional norm of ability. There are obviously negative consequences of the medicalization of patients and the use of a biomedical model in the definition of disability and in regimes of rehabilitation. The emphasis on ability and activism in the dominant culture and the contributory model of rights may be particularly prominent in American society, in which youth culture has especially valued beauty, individualism, achievement, and success. Youthfulness, dexterity, and agility become the principal criteria for the aesthetic evaluation of people by reference to their bodies. Consequently, an ideology of "ableism" underpins more general values about the social importance of sports, athleticism, and masculinity, and the idea of physical dexterity becomes an index of more general social distinction. In contemporary consumer societies, the youthful and powerful body has increasingly become the sign of social worth: the body has become a dominant theme in the notion of the self as a project. Obesity is regarded as personal failure and weakness, whereas weight loss is a mark of self-control and responsibility.

In terms of the sociology of knowledge, "disability"—not unlike notions of "intelligence," "race," and "gender"—has been "deconstructed" by social movements employing the politics of the theory of social construction. The Union of the Physically Impaired Against Segregation defines disability in terms of social citizenship as a loss of social and political opportunities. The social model of disability is thus highly appropriate for advocacy purposes, because it forces us to attend to inadequate social provision. The disability movement has employed a social model of disability as a direct challenge to the medical model, in which disease and sickness are produced by a specific entity (such as a virus or bacterium). The medical model does not consider the subjective worldview of patients as constitutive of the condition and does not recognize the role of politics and culture in shaping human illness. By concentrating on the ways in which disability is socially produced, the social model has succeeded in shifting political debate away from a narrow agenda dominated by biomedicine to discourses about rights (Albrecht 1992).

While the constructionist approach is therefore important in political campaigns and advocacy work, it is not entirely satisfactory from an intellectual point of view. Without some assumptions that impairment involves some real damage to the physical body, it is difficult to see how it is possible to argue that disability is a loss of rights. The social constructionist debate raises the question of *what* is being socially constructed. Indeed, extreme versions of constructionist theory appear to deny that there is any phenomenon to be constructed. Is it impairment, the physical condition, that is constructed through social definition? Without some idea of physical impairment, it is difficult to develop an assumption about the common vulnerability of people as such. People with impairment are disabled because in an "ableist culture" they suffer from a lack of rights, but this does not mean we can ignore the physical or embodied dimensions of their pain and vulnerability.

Attempts to deconstruct the hegemonic paradigms of social control typically ignore as irrelevant or reject as misleading the subjective experiences of the individuals who get labeled as mad or neurotic or incompetent or disabled (Weinberg 2005). Critical theories of insanity, because they concentrate on the study of the *conditions* that produce interpretation or knowledge (such as the history of psychiatric labels), do not address the phenomenological *character* of madness—or addiction, or illness, or deviance. We need to attend, then, to another question: What is this *thing* called disability? The question invites us to consider more seriously the phenomenological richness of the condition itself. The disabled child may suffer from a loss of rights, but what is the phenomenology of the child's experience? Social constructionist approaches tend to close off any inquiry into the everyday experience of, for example, the limbless thalidomide child. Furthermore, how shall we promote the rights of those with disabilities or special needs if we are not prepared to acknowledge the very obduracy of those disabilities or special needs? The strict constructionist argument sometimes seems to imply that if we can simply persuade ourselves and significant others that our disabilities are merely conventional or constructed, then so they shall be. This idealist conclusion is not morally or philosophically convincing for those who know that transforming and overcoming psychological affliction or physical impairment amounts to much more than changing our beliefs or the dominant language of welfare bureaucracies. Social constructionist theory ignores the very vulnerability that constitutes the everyday world of the impaired.

A democratic ethos behind social constructionist arguments encourages us to assume that if only the social definition of the situation could be changed, then we could all be transformed or reconstituted. Yet we must, with a view to the importance of the sociology of the body, take note of what I want to call the "stuffness" of life—that is, its overwhelming "quiddity." For the sociological imagination, "quiddity" is a word that has useful etymological properties. It can refer to more or less useless debates about whether things exist. "To quiddle" is to engage in trifling debate. Alternatively, it refers to the very nature of a thing: a quid is that which a thing is. The reality of the everyday world in which we live is forced upon us because we can touch, smell, feel, and occasionally eat it. While idealist philosophers might discuss the reality of the everyday world, we still have to live in it. Debates about epistemology are necessary in philosophy, but they have no place in the everyday world, where we have to cope with hungry infants, disorderly teenagers, or disoriented elders. Similarly, while medical historians might be interested in the evolution of diabetes as a classificatory label, such debates are unhelpful to a person who has to manage the impairments—high blood pressure and blindness— that may attend the condition.

Social construction as a theory cannot effectively deal with the stuffness or quiddity of discomfort. We are vulnerable, and these disturbances of everyday life—in effect, the human condition—are manifest in the discomfort, pains, and tribulations of everyday life and the obdurate quality of the "thingness" of existence. Vulnerability may be socially constructed because our values of youthfulness, activism, and ability tend to marginalize people with impairments, but the theory of social construction should not encourage us to adopt an idealist stance that physical and mental impairments have no phenomenological reality. Deafness may involve a loss of social rights, but it is, to coin an expression, a quiddable condition. The unintended moral consequence of social construction may be to blind us to the misery that constitutes the human community out of a common experience of ordinary suffering.

MENTAL HEALTH, LEARNING DIFFICULTIES, AND SOCIAL INCLUSION

We have seen that disability is a condition that departs from the normalizing aspects of the contributory model of citizenship. Disability illustrates the point that membership in an associational democracy is rather like membership in a club. Membership is itself a resource or asset that distinguishes insiders from outsiders. Social citizenship rewards those who are "normal" members (particularly people who work, have families, and do not suffer from any impairment). While this is true of physical impairment, it is even more pronounced in the case of mental health and learning difficulties. The problem of intelligence and learning disability crucially brings out the limitations of Jürgen Habermas's model of civil society, in which effective participation in debate and discussion in the public sphere assumes communicative competence. The sociology of mental health provides an interesting platform from which to examine the rationalist assumptions of Habermas's communicative model of social life. In his influential *Structural Transformation of the Public Sphere,* Habermas (1989) traced the rise and fall of the bourgeois public sphere. This study has been central to the sociological and philosophical analysis of the public domain, and rightly so, but the debate has so far failed to recognize that the bourgeois actors who enter this sphere are assumed to be physically and mentally able. The whole rationalist debate about membership in the public sphere involves a set of assumptions about human ability and capacity—that is, "ableism"—that are often inappropriate, given the levels of impairment in the community, levels that are rising as populations age. In the rationalist model of politics, the social participants are, by implication, essentially young, literate, intelligent, and able. In short, Habermas's rational Enlightenment model does not recognize vulnerability as an issue.

Michel Foucault was a trenchant critic of the underlying notions of rationality that have played an important role in the medical and legal normalization of the deviant. The major debate of postwar social science has, in retrospect, occurred between Habermasian rationalism and post-structuralism over the status of language and reason, the political implications of relativism, and the nature of inclusion in modern society. Theories of communication have become dominant in modern social science, because those who can communicate rationally and effectively can play a normal part in civil society (as a space of communicative rationality). It has been claimed, particularly by sociologists, that the norm of communicative competence can function as a criterion of inclusion and exclusion, and they have turned to such issues as gender, disability, insanity, and addiction to examine the processes of exclusion in modern societies that emphasize activism, reflexivity, and rationality in social participation. The underlying concept of the "active citizen" may also carry notions about physical as much as communicative ability and competence. Given the centrality of the issue of rationality, especially communicative rationality, it is important to think about the implications of so-called learning disabilities or learning difficulties in relation to the model of the active, rationally competent citizen. Foucault's historical studies of power and knowledge have been recognized as particularly pertinent to understanding modern processes of exclusion, especially those relating, for example, to old age. (The rise of gerontology and geriatric medicine has been interpreted as indicative of changing power relations with respect to aging processes in modern societies, where the elderly are increasingly seen to be problematic.)

Foucault's argument in *Madness and Civilization* (1971) is that the dialogue between Folly and Reason that was central to the Shakespearian notion of madness in *King Lear* has been terminated by the Cartesian *cogito ergo sum*, and that in the age of reason, insanity is banished from normal society by the creation of asylums and the seclusion of the insane. This argument laid the foundations for a more general

proposal that the history of ideas should consider the relationship between power and knowledge and that we should understand the functions of the state under the general concept of "governmentality." The
modern form of government requires the exclusion of the possibility
that reason might be contaminated by madness and insists that the
citizen, as the able-bodied employee, should not be distracted by the
lame, the sick, and the unemployable. The age of the contributory
right—that is, the emergence of modern citizenship on the historical
stage—opened with the medical exclusion of the unfit and the insane.
A citizen is assumed to be an able-bodied person with a voice to express interests in a public sphere that is open to rational debate between contending parties.

My discussion so far has been primarily concerned with the implications of physical impairment. "Learning difficulty" raises important
but different problems and issues. The concept of learning disability
includes people with a significantly reduced capacity to understand
new or complex information, to learn new skills, and to cope independently. These individuals suffer from an impaired social functioning
that leaves them dependent on others. Such disabilities normally start
before adulthood, with lasting effects on subsequent development.
This obviously broad definition refers to a heterogeneous population.
It has, in fact, two components—an IQ element and a social-behavioral
dimension. An IQ of below seventy does not immediately classify
somebody as suffering from a learning disability. People with autism
often have high intelligence. The category is further complicated by
the fact that people with learning disabilities often also have physical
or sensory impairment. It is estimated that in England and Wales,
210,000 people suffer from a severe learning difficulty and 1.2 million
(25 per 1,000 people) have a moderate learning difficulty.

Mental health and learning disabilities are deeply stigmatized. The
word "imbecile" (from the Latin *imbecillus*) refers to people who are
physically weak or feeble, mentally weak, or of weak character. In 1802
it referred to a person of weak intellect. The phrase "simple-minded,"
occurring in 1744, meant that a person possessed little or no subtlety
of mind, or referred to a feeble or weak-minded person. A "simpleton"
in 1650 was one who was deficient in sense or intellect. Now, models

of citizenship, like models of economic action, presuppose intelligent and rational agents who are capable of understanding and articulating their own interests and needs. Adult citizens can read about and generally understand their legal entitlements. It is assumed that they are capable of undertaking collective and individual action to express their needs and achieve desired outcomes. The notion of an "active citizen" assumes effective and rational agency, and hence the idea of communicative competence marks a presumption about the intellectual capacities of a rights-bearing agent. Despite the importance of the concept of communication to any understanding of rationality in critical social theory, the problems, for example, of Alzheimer's disease in the aging process and of learning disabilities for the practical competence of citizens discursively engaging in the public domain have not been adequately considered as problems of citizenship.

People with severe or moderate learning disabilities have difficulties expressing or articulating their own interests and needs. While the deaf and dumb have sign language, it is difficult to assess how much people with learning difficulties actually understand, or what their needs are. Deaf people have been able to establish a range of rights that express their interests, but the mobilization of people with learning disabilities encounters severe limitations in terms of their political involvement. More problematically, it is difficult for people without a learning disability to know with any confidence what people with learning disabilities need. Their needs have to be interpreted by people who are competent. In the case of learning difficulty, the role of helpers and carers becomes crucial. People with severe learning disabilities might engage with society by proxy—that is, through the interpretative activities of caregivers who become expert in facilitating the communication of people with such disabilities. Yet because learning disability is profoundly stigmatized, social psychologists have found that people are reluctant to identify with the label; the political organization of people with learning disabilities is thus limited by the stigmatic label itself. The phrase "learning difficulty" is interesting because it obviously attempts to avoid the pejorative implications of everyday terms for persons of poor intelligence. It suggests a problem of communication, a condition that gives rise to social embarrassment or discomfort. It implies a judgment about interactional competence, and it also suggests that the condition could be managed or improved. "Difficulty" can be overcome through training. It suggests, in particular, a defect of communicative competence or rationality. It is not an illness, and it rejects the comparison with "physical disability."

JUSTICE AND NATURAL TALENT

Citizenship confers status and identity to members of a political community. As modern societies become more diverse with the growth of labor migration, the flow of refugees, and the increase in asylum seekers, questions of identity or "identity politics" take a central place in contemporary citizenship. The traditional issues of economic citizenship—safety at work, full employment, access to union membership, the right to strike, retirement, and security of pension rights—continue to be important aspects of social policy, but new issues concerning cultural identity now shape what has been called "cultural citizenship." Disability politics belongs to a wider category of representation that political scientists have called "ascriptive identity groups," groups that organize around characteristics that individuals cannot or do not freely choose, such as ethnicity or age. Political identification by ascription creates important problems of representation. For example, people with learning difficulties may not want to accept the label that creates the basis of ascription.

Disability has also become an issue in identity politics and cultural citizenship, because the disability movement has questioned the taken-for-granted assumptions about equality and participation that historically underpinned Marshallian citizenship. Critics of the universal social rights model argue that universal assumptions and expectations about equality cannot be delivered by modern states, and, furthermore, that these assumptions cannot address the special needs of particular social groups. We need a differentiated, not uniform, model of citizenship. Achieving standardized equality of outcomes or opportunities may be neither feasible nor desirable, and hence fairness of treatment rather than equality of outcome may be more relevant to differentiated citizenship. Although this argument has been directed primarily toward the inclusion of ethnic minorities, it applies with equal force to the politics of disability.

Political philosophers such as John Rawls and Ronald Dworkin have argued that equality of opportunity only makes sense if people start life with the same or similar resources and chances. The "difference principle" is that naturally talented people should have higher incomes, but these inequalities are justified if they are part of a system in which their higher wages benefit the least advantaged members of society (Rawls 1971). Societies are fair if a person's fate is determined by choice rather than by circumstance. The point is that disabilities are not chosen by people, and hence the disadvantages that attend impairment and disability can never be justified. Theories of equal opportunity have primarily concentrated on the arbitrary nature of gender and race in determining people's life chances. More recently, attention has turned to the role of "natural talents" in the distribution of social rewards. Very talented athletes should, for example, be rewarded for their skills and training by winning competitions. The same arguments might apply to the social competition for wages and other economic rewards. But what is a natural talent? Demographic research shows that the members of higher socioeconomic groups have longer life expectancy, lower morbidity, and lower infant mortality than lower socioeconomic groups. Generally speaking, rich people are taller than poor people, because diet and genetic legacy play an important part in the determination of height. Therefore, natural talents are real talents, but this does not necessarily mean that they are produced by nature without the mediation of society.

The "natural lottery" is unfair, if we assume that all human beings have equal moral worth. Citizenship mitigates the social consequences of the arbitrary lottery of nature. It exists to ensure that some level of equality can be achieved—for example, through some redistribution of resources through the collective sharing of wealth. Yet what are the grounds upon which we can justify the claim that all human beings are morally equal? Philosophers have traditionally claimed either that equal moral worth has to be justified by religious arguments (we are all equal in the eyes of God), or by reference to natural law (we are equal in terms of an ideal notion of nature), or by a theory of a social contract (we were all equal in a state of nature before the existence of social inequalities). These three principles of justification often present problems in secular societies where belief in a personal God, nature, or a social contract may not be widespread. The argument about human vulnerability suggests a possible solution. We are all equal in the sense that we are all vulnerable over the life course in terms of the arbitrary contingencies of human existence. Society should be organized to protect those individuals whose lives are the most precarious in order to achieve some fair distribution of resources.

CONCLUSION: RIGHTS TO HEALTH OR TO HEALTH CARE?

Despite improvements in recognizing the rights of people with disability and impairment, social citizenship has failed as a mechanism of recognition and redistribution. This failure of national forms of welfare has created opportunities for the development of global responses, especially through the legal instrument of human rights. The Declaration on the Rights of Mentally Retarded Persons (United Nations 1971), the Declaration on the Rights of Disabled Persons (United Nations 1975), and the World Programme of Action Concerning Disabled Persons (United Nations 1982) indicate an emerging global discourse of rights for disability. Human rights discourse is a promising arena for the development of rights for disabled persons, because such rights are based on concepts of human dignity and vulnerability, not on the notion that entitlement must be based on duty and contribution. Whereas the social rights of national citizenship often depend on an assumption about the able-bodied individual, human rights are primarily based on an idea of human vulnerability that we all share—not as workers, but as human beings.

We often refer to the rights of disabled people under the general rubric of "health rights," but these are difficult to define. Article 12 of the International Covenant on Economic, Social, and Cultural Rights recognizes everyone's right to the enjoyment of the highest attainable standard of physical and mental health. The Article notes that states must take steps to reduce infant mortality, improve the environment, control epidemics, and make adequate provision of health services. There is widespread skepticism that a health right can be coherently defined, however, because the right to health is not a right to be healthy. Because there is an important aspect of genetic inheritance in human illness (such as diabetes, Huntington's disease, or Down syndrome), it is difficult to enforce a health right retrospectively. Illness and disability are, in part, a function of aging, and hence there are life cycle issues that are relevant to forming health rights. In addition, there are important differences between men and women in terms of sexual function, and no set of legal provisions can entirely ignore such differences. Women have children and lactate; men do not. Men and women also differ considerably in terms of self-reported health status (Turner 2004, 303). Because it is possible to distinguish between health and subjective or self-reported health, it would be difficult to legislate for subjective health satisfaction.

Some authors have attempted to define a right to health by reference to some international consensus on health issues or by reference to the empowerment of individuals. Rights to health care rather than to health itself offer a more practical strategy that can monitor states that fail to maintain conditions promoting health. Many people may not be able to enjoy healthy lives as a result of the natural lottery, but human rights provisions can constrain governments to meet certain minimum conditions of health care. Human rights thus compensate for the inequalities of the natural lottery, just as citizenship compensated historically for the inequalities of the social lottery. Human rights, because they are not tied to contribution or obligation, offer some protection to those who are burdened by the injustices of nature.

RIGHTS OF THE BODY

INTRODUCTION: HEALTH AND SOCIAL RIGHTS

A minimum level of good health is a material precondition for the enjoyment of human rights. We might interpret this commonsense observation through the political economy of Karl Marx against the claims of liberalism and its assumptions about individual rights. Marx believed that democratic institutions in capitalism had failed because the social dominance of the ruling class was based on its ownership and control of the economic foundations of society. Marx argued in *On the Jewish Question* that the emancipation of the Jews as a consequence of the French Revolution and the granting of equal rights was based on an artificial division between social and political life. Only through an economic transformation of society could citizens effectively enjoy the benefits of civil rights. Marx's sociological argument lurks behind most contemporary interpretations of the importance of improving social and economic conditions to make political rights meaningful. This primacy of the socioeconomic conditions of civil society over political rights is illustrated, for example, by the emphasis on labor laws in protecting working people from economic exploitation (Woodiwiss 1998). In more specific terms, this argument is framed by the distinction between the International Covenant on Civil and Political Rights, on the one hand, and by the International Covenant on Economic, Social, and Cultural Rights on the other.

This distinction is fundamental. One can either argue that the right to have rights is the political and legal foundation of all claims to rights, or one can take Marx's position that civil rights are merely ideological notions if they are not supported by real economic and social resources. A sociology of rights attends to the social and economic foundations of rights, in which the protection of human vulnerability is the key component of human rights. In short, possession of adequate economic resources is critical to good health, and good health is critical to the enjoyment of rights. Income equality and effective participation in social institutions are the two components of what we might call "health citizenship," namely, the rights to health care, a safe environment, clean water, and an adequate food supply (Turner 2004). Sociology thus has an obvious point of entry into the study of human rights: How can we understand, empirically, the conditions that make possible Article 3, in which "everyone has the right to life, liberty and security of person"?

Public health research suggests that the conditions of good health are a minimum level of income, education, access to health care, and social attachments that offer a sense of personal dignity and self-respect. The final condition is based on the finding that, without social attachments or social capital, people engage in activities that are self-destructive (such as substance abuse, self-harm, and eventually suicide). Health and illness depend on two dimensions of vulnerability, the physical and the psychological. (There is an important connection here between environmentalism, green politics, and human vulnerability.) The sociology of human rights explores the connections between our ontological vulnerability, the precariousness of the institutions of civil society, and the problem of economic scarcity. Sociology further comprehends these causal connections through the study of war, famine, and pestilence, and there is a sense in which the sociology of rights involves an application of a neo-Malthusian perspective. This study of human rights has argued that structural causes of new wars and attendant political fanaticism include overpopulation, state failure, unsatisfied expectations, poverty, and the erosion of civil society, and that these structural conditions are further fueled by Hollywood ideologies of celebrity and masculinity and technologically equipped by the availability of cheap but efficient armaments.

This extended essay on human rights has argued that our common vulnerability underpins human rights and provides a stance against cultural relativism and nihilism. Various claims against this understanding of vulnerability have been considered, but the most intriguing is the position that suggests that our vulnerability is itself a contextual and historical variable. For instance, improvements in medical science and technology in the last two decades have demonstrated that the biological conditions that cause vulnerability could be controlled (and, some would argue, eliminated). We need to consider two variations on this position. The first is the perfectly reasonable argument that improvements in science and its technological applications will allow human beings to circumscribe their vulnerability and hence reduce its impact on morbidity and mortality. Quite simply, life can improve. Let us take the example of suicide. In Western societies, we might take the view that suicide, especially in young men, is an expression of the vulnerability of youth. Yet in recent years, suicide rates have been declining in many advanced societies by improvements in ambulance services, emergency care, accident treatment, psychological counseling, and post-traumatic nursing. Modern medicine makes it less likely that we can commit suicide successfully, and in this sense, medical interventions can be said to reduce human vulnerability. The other argument is the utopian proposition that, given current improvements in genetic research (specifically stem-cell research) and overall improvements in medical care, we can live forever. Vulnerability becomes irrelevant.

What are the implications of these arguments for human rights theory and practice? What is the relationship between medical sciences and the enjoyment of human rights? The development of NRTS, genetic engineering, and the enhancement of human traits point toward a "second medical revolution" that combines microbiology and informational science. This revolution clearly presents a major challenge to traditional institutions and religious cosmologies, but it may also pose a threat to the processes of political governance. The modern sociological notion of the "risk society" invites questions about the unintended consequences of medical change, about whether the technological imperative can be regulated, and about the relationships between pure research, commercialization, and academic autonomy. New medical technologies have major implications for social control (in the use, for example, of DNA testing in forensic criminology and insurance work) and for the management of human reproduction. In thinking about these problems, social scientists have often turned to the dystopian visions of society offered by Aldous Huxley in *Brave New World,* originally published in 1932, and by George Orwell in *Nineteen Eighty-four* (1949). Whereas Orwell's dystopia described a totalitarian regime that employed information technology to suppress political opposition through centralized political regulation, Huxley imagined a regime that employed biotechnology (genetic manipulation, psychoactive drugs, and high-tech amusements) to achieve social order through cultural standardization and mediocrity, inducing hedonistic contentment in its citizens. If the Orwellian society of 1984 perfected direct repression, the brave new world planned a social paradise—or at least a Disneyland version of a secular paradise. In the language of modern sociology, Huxley envisioned social integration achieved through the medicalization of social problems and by the development of a leisure society and consumer culture.

UTOPIAN HEALTH

These dystopian manifestos of our political future are particularly relevant to any discussion of human rights, social control, and medical science. The increasing dependence of advanced societies on antidepressant drugs has been a common topic of social criticism for some decades. The newer antidepressants were originally welcomed by the public as safe alternatives to tricyclic antidepressants. (It is virtually impossible for a person to overdose deliberately on new antidepressants.) As a consequence, Prozac prospered in the United States as a major lifestyle drug. The side effects and social problems of dependence on drugs that once promised to provide us happiness are now well known (Kramer 1994), however, and the contemporary global spread of crack and Ecstasy in youth cultures has reaffirmed the relevance of Huxley's fiction for understanding the social problems of advanced societies. The second medical revolution has raised even more profound political questions about addiction, dependency, and social control.

For some authors, the rationality of science, new developments in biotechnology, and their applications to improving health are compatible with the liberal values of American democracy (Kass 2002). Why, then, do advances in biotechnology seem to be a problem? One answer is that contemporary medical science has the unintended consequence of eroding the very social meanings that make any society possible. Science and technology are aspects of modern secularization that, by offering pragmatic and practical solutions to human relations, demystify traditional values that underpin everyday life. For example, contemporary applications of microbiological sciences to reproduction have created "extra-corporeal fertilization" or "asexual reproduction" with far-reaching, if unanticipated, consequences for fundamental social relations, such as parenthood. In more simple terms, technology has severed the natural connection between sexual intercourse and human reproduction. Because successful reproduction outside the womb may become possible in the future, technology fundamentally challenges the basic meanings of generation, regeneration, and parenthood. Parenting, of course, is a social process that is important for social citizenship, political identity, adulthood, and civic responsibility, so the implications of biological science for civil and human rights are troublesome. Technological advances and the commodification of reproduction through the commercial exploitation of donors have significant implications for sexual relationships and parenthood—and hence for religious understandings of life. If lesbian parenthood is already with us through adoption, surrogacy, and sperm donation, then gay parenthood is not far away through the invention of extra-corporeal fertility techniques. The benefits of "therapeutic cloning" for inherited disease may create the conditions whereby "designer babies" become a routine aspect of reproduction.

In many respects, cloning can be seen as merely an extension of the issues related to assisted reproduction. While many governments are concerned about the dramatic implications of human cloning, the idea of "therapeutic cloning" continues to be attractive, but this may be, as it were, the back door to full-scale human cloning. Therapeutic cloning employs animal or human tissue to clone whole organs, such as hearts, lungs, and kidneys, that can then be used in therapeutic organ transplants. Stem-cell research on the human embryo holds out the possibility of discovering effective cures for diabetes, Parkinson's disease, and Alzheimer's disease, but many conservative critics have condemned this type of research. The National Conference of Catholic Bishops, for instance, lobbied the U.S. Congress to block funding for such research. Stem-cell research looks beneficial, but many religious leaders fear that it is impossible to prevent therapeutic cloning becoming the slippery slope leading to the eventual cloning of humans.

Sociologists need to take NRTS seriously, because they will change the nature and functions of kinship relationships. The basic issue behind these new technologies is that, in separating sexual intercourse from biological reproduction, they implicitly bring into question the conventional social roles of husbands and wives, fathers and mothers, as necessary in reproduction. Indeed, such technologies make a range of new social relationships in reproductive arrangements possible. For instance, donations of egg and sperm can come from people who are already dead, and hence a child may never have access to his or her biological parents. The new technologies open up novel social relations that go well beyond surrogacy and adoption. When science separates sex and reproduction, it is difficult to determine who the mother is. Is she the donor of the egg, the surrogate mother who carries and delivers, or the parent who brings up and cares for the child? As noted above, in a number of European countries, new technologies are now helping women reproduce into their sixties, and it is unclear who will take responsibility for the long-term care of their children. It is conceivable that medical scientists could construct an artificial womb that would allow a homosexual male couple to reproduce without the assistance of a woman as a surrogate mother. These technological advances are not effectively regulated by law or by professional consensus.

The social consequences of this second medical revolution will be dramatic, and the new biology will generate far-reaching social con-flicts in policy formation, politics, and law. These innovations in medi-cal technology have a direct relevance to human rights. Article 16 says, "Men and women of full age, without limitation due to race, national-ity or religion, have the right to marry and to found a family," but medical sciences are bringing about radical changes to family life in the long run. The more complex issue is that medical science is trans-forming the relationship between the self, the body, and society. Who will, under these new circumstances, have legal ownership of the human body? Should people be free to sell parts of their bodies for commercial gain? Can couples produce offspring that could virtually be used as "spare parts" for future surgery? Could families or societies develop a bank of genetic material in which they would invest "genetic capital" from which they could draw down biological investments in time of future need? These questions have already become an impor-tant aspect of the debate about the ethics of organ exchange, organ transplants, and assisted reproduction.

Medical technology and microbiology hold out the promise—through the Human Genome Project, therapeutic cloning, transplants, "wonder drugs," nanotechnology, and microsurgery—of freedom from aging, infirmity, and disability. Cosmetic surgery promises to restore the body and give us an eternally youthful exterior. These med-ical possibilities have produced utopian visions of a world free from disease—a new mirage of health in which the human body will come to stand in an entirely new relationship to self and society. These changes create further opportunities for the development of a global medical system of governance in which medicine may exercise an ex-panded power over life and death. National governments have yet to take seriously the issue of adequate legislative regulation of this global medical system.

The problem with Huxley's vision of democracy is that while we (or most of us) will be happier and healthier, we will no longer neces-sarily be human in the conventional sense of being the natural off-spring of human heterosexual parents, who are, broadly speaking, our contemporaries. Francis Fukuyama in *Our Posthuman Future* (2002) has considered the political implications of the sciences of the brain, neuropharmacology and the medical control of behavior, the prolongation of life, and genetic engineering. Being less concerned with ethical arguments about dehumanization and more concerned with the social and political implications of the "new geneticism," Fukuyama believes that political and legal regulation is required to manage scientific innovations and their commercial exploitation. While the biotechnology industry and the community of research scholars are generally against regulation, he favors regulation in the hope that we may avoid replicating past pharmaceutical catastrophes, such as those associated with Elixir Sulfanilamide and thalidomide, or avoid other social disasters such as bovine spongiform encephalopathy and Creutzfeldt-Jakob disease. Regulation is, however, difficult to achieve, and direct prohibitions are almost impossible to enforce and dangerous to scientific freedom (especially to so-called curiosity-driven research). While legislative prohibition is generally ineffective and counterproductive, Kass (2002) argues that federal funding should not be available to promote morally hazardous in vitro fertilization and embryonic research.

REGULATION AND REPRODUCTIVE CHOICE

There is a fundamental problem behind the legislative effort to regulate biomedicine and biotechnology: What are the reproductive rights that require definition and protection? Is there a universal right to reproduce? The 1994 International Conference on Population and Development adopted a definition of reproductive health asserting that people have a right to reproduce and the individual freedom to decide when and how often. The recommendations of the Conference established three requirements of reproductive health: every sex act should be free, intended, and healthy. Reproductive freedom may come to be generously interpreted as each person's right to have a child of his or her own choosing by whatever means and at whatever cost. Yet rights to reproduce could not be individual rights, because they could not be exercised alone. Reproduction clearly affects children and parents, and hence reproductive rights are not necessarily individual rights. While we might easily accept the notion that rape is a violent infringement of a reproductive right, is involuntary infertility a ground for rights-claims against the state for medical assistance? Can a childless woman in her late fifties or early sixties legitimately claim a right of access to NRTS, free of charge, in a nationalized welfare system, or should we simply allow the market to allocate scarce resources according to demand? In a market economy, rich women of mature age would have reproductive rights, or at least access to adequate health care, but these benefits might be denied to younger, economically poorer women.

The underlying problem of reproductive rights is the relationship between parents and their offspring. If there is a reproductive right, then we could assume a reproductive obligation is to secure the best future for children, including not only economic support but also intimacy and care. The argument against reproductive assistance to the elderly is that they cannot reasonably guarantee such supports. In a sense, geriatric mothers would be condemning their offspring to a future as orphans. A reproductive obligation might also include securing the best health of the child, and there would thus be arguments against permitting or encouraging disabled and impaired couples to reproduce where there is a known high probability that their children may inherit impairment. These arguments are deeply problematic. Can one discriminate against people who suffer from disabilities by arguing that they should refrain from reproduction? Where would one draw the line? Are diabetes, deafness, and dwarfism grounds for the curtailment of reproductive rights, along with devastating conditions such as Huntington's chorea? It is unclear, too, how such reproductive claims and obligations might be enforced without compulsion. In a democratic culture, one might balk at the idea of compulsory sterilization because it is a gross infringement of individual rights. Would we allow unrestricted decisions about reproduction (including cloning) under all circumstances, though? Should women who are HIV positive be allowed to reproduce freely? Is the right to abortion a universal reproductive liberty?

The language of rights implies human agency; that is, human beings have the capacity to choose between different courses of action. If I have a legitimate claim, then it is assumed that I have the ability to choose to fulfill the obligations that come with that claim. Rights language also implies a language of volition and responsibility. Infringements suggest the possibility of guilt and punishment. Genetic engineering and the use of genetic science for forensic purposes raise far-reaching difficulties for liberties in a modern democracy. The applications of genetic science in forensic investigations of terrorists are likely to be welcomed by the public, but the implications of applied genetics are radical, and the consequences, uncertain. There has been considerable discussion in the media concerning the discovery of a "gene" for criminal behavior, for example. Without questioning the scientific credibility of such claims, these developments represent a further medicalization of society, in which the discourse of surveillance and control replaces that of responsibility and liability. It has long been recognized, at least since the development of positivist criminology, that behavioral accounts of human action involve reductionism and preclude any evaluation of rational responsibility. These arguments about rights ultimately require an account of human nature. They thus require normative justifications that can resolve the problems of cultural relativism.

The notion of human dignity is clearly important in the formulation of standards by which governments might regulate or attempt to regulate science with regard to reproduction. Still, one political problem remains worryingly implicit. The new biotechnology involves the emergence of a new eugenics. Biotechnology is forcing modern states to develop eugenics policies that will somehow address the new challenges of asexual reproduction. At one level, eugenics is simply any human strategy to improve reproduction. The term "eu-genesis" refers, according to the Oxford English Dictionary, to "the quality of breeding well and freely," and "eugenic" (relating to "the production of fine offspring") first appeared in 1833. The eugenics of the 1930s, associated with authoritarian regimes, has been widely condemned as a gross denial of individual freedom. We might say that if fascist eugenics reflected compulsory state policies, postwar eugenics has been individualistic and discretionary. Any policy that influences reproduction can be described as "eugenic," however. For example, handing out free contraceptives or giving contraceptive advice to schoolchildren is a eugenic practice. Fascist eugenics was a policy of public regulation of breeding, and in modern times, the one-child family policy of the Chinese government has been a draconian method to reduce population growth. By contrast, most liberal societies have regarded reproduction as a private issue over which the state and the law should not interfere, at least directly and overtly.

Because the sex act is still regarded as a private choice, states and their legislatures have been reluctant to regard reproductive activity as a public concern. States have in the past attempted to control the spread of sexually transmitted diseases among the military and have waged educational campaigns to promote the use of condoms, but Western democratic states have been loath to use criminal law, for example, to control the spread of HIV/AIDS. The idea that the state might need to regulate reproduction is seen to be a fulfillment of Huxley's *Brave New World*. The separation of private sex acts from reproduction by technology does complicate the legal issue. Do individuals (heterosexual, gay, or lesbian) have a right to reproduce by whatever technological means possible, regardless of the future implications for social identities and relationships? Such questions bear disturbing implications because we have neither convincing answers nor the institutional means to enforce whatever answers we might eventually discover. The status of cloning is a powerful inducement to scientists in unregulated environments to press ahead in the competition to perfect human cloning, therapeutic or otherwise. In this competitive global field, biotechnological advances continue without effective control or direction.

CAN WE LIVE FOREVER?

Academic debates about the right to reproduce have specifically addressed the broad implications of cloning and artificial reproduction for human rights. One emerging issue is even more problematic, however, and it concerns the consequences of medical science for aging. In traditional societies, the relationship between resources (especially the food supply) and life expectancy was, more or less, regulated by a Malthusian logic. Classical economics was associated with the demographic theories of Thomas Malthus (1766–1834), who, in *Essay on the Principle of Population as It Affects the Future Improvement of Society* (1798), argued that the increase in population would inevitably supersede the food supply, given the sexual drive, the need for food, and the declining yield of the soil. Population increase could either be controlled by positive means (such as famine, disease, and war) or by preventative means (such as vice, chastity, and late marriage). Any attempt to improve the living conditions of the working class could not be sustained in the long term, because such reforms would increase the population, thereby reducing living standards by reducing the food supply.

History does not appear to have supported this Malthusian pessimism. For example, in Britain, the invention of modern contraception in the 1820s, the expansion of the food supply through colonialism, and technical improvements in agricultural production controlled reproduction and expanded the supply of resources. With improvements in nutrition, food supply and distribution, water supply, sanitation, and housing, the death rate fell, but the increase in population was supported by improvements in agriculture. Eventually the birth rate also fell, as life expectancy increased with the decline of childhood illness (such as whooping cough). Yet the possibility of extending life expectancy in the rich societies of the North through the application of medical research on stem cells has clear Malthusian implications for the world as a whole—and because there is a very close relationship between poverty and injustice, we should take this Malthusian question seriously if we hope to understand the relationship between rights and poverty.

It is unclear what causes aging. Medical interest in aging goes back at least to writers such as Luigi Cornaro (1464–1566). In his *Discourses on the Temperate Life,* Cornaro argued that his own longevity was a consequence of temperance, exercise, and a good diet. The body's finite supply of vital spirits could be husbanded by temperate ways. The idea that aging is inevitable has been the basic presupposition of gerontology ever since. If aging is an inevitable process of cellular degeneration, then the question of whether we have a right to live forever does not arise (apart from fanciful speculation). Obviously, life expectancy increased dramatically in the late nineteenth and twentieth centuries, but in the second half of the twentieth century, it had reached a plateau. If we take men in the United Kingdom, the expectation of life at birth in 1901 was only 45.5 years, but by 1991 this was 73.2 years. Subsequent demographic data, however, indicate only a modest increase from 75.4 in 2001 to a projected 77.6 by 2020. Although this change in life expectancy represents a huge leap from the situation in 1901, the rate of change is no longer dramatic.

In conventional gerontology, the question of living forever might, in practical terms, mean living a full life and achieving the average expectation of longevity. More recently, though, there has been considerable speculation as to whether medical science could reverse the aging process. Between the 1960s and 1980s, biologists held that normal cells had a "replicative senescence"; that is, normal tissues could only divide a finite number of times before entering a stage of quiescence (Hayflick 1982). Cells were observed in vitro in a process of natural senescence, and eventually experiments in vivo established a distinction between normal and pathological cells in terms of cellular division (Shostak 2002). Pathological cells appeared, paradoxically, to have no necessary limitation on replication. Therefore, "immortalization" was the distinctive feature of a pathological cell line. Biologists extrapolated that finite cell division meant that the aging of the whole organism was inevitable. These laboratory findings confirmed the view that human life had an intrinsic, predetermined limit, and that through pathological developments some cells might avoid the otherwise inescapable senescence of cellular life.

This framework of aging was eventually disrupted by the discovery that human embryonic cells were capable of continuous division in culture and showed no sign of any inevitable replicative crisis. Certain non-pathological cells (or stem cells) were capable of indefinite division and hence were "immortalized." The cultivation of these cells as an experimental form of life has challenged existing assumptions about the boundaries between the normal and the pathological—and between life and death. Stem-cell research begins to define the arena within which the body has reserves of renewable tissue, and it suggests that the limits of biological growth are not fixed or inflexible.

The body has a surplus of stem cells capable of survival beyond the death of the organism. With these developments in "micro-bio-gerontology," regenerative medicine's capacity to expand the limits of life becomes a plausible prospect. This new interpretation of replication locates aging as a shifting threshold between surplus and waste, or between obsolescence and renewal.

Because World Bank economists see the aging of the developed world as a threat to global economic growth, there is much excitement about the commercial possibilities of stem-cell research as an aspect of regenerative medicine. Companies operating in the Caribbean and Asia are already offering regenerative medicine as part of a holiday package designed to alleviate the negative consequences of degenerative diseases such as multiple sclerosis or diabetes. Regenerative medicine, developed from research into rejuvenating aging stem cells, promises to heal broken bones, bad burns, blindness, deafness, heart damage, and Parkinson's disease. (It is based on the notion of "Strategies for Engineered Negligible Senescence.") The idea of geriatric tourism might become an addendum to sexual tourism in the world of advanced biocapitalism. One sign of the times was an academic event hosted by the Cambridge University Life Extension and Rejuvenation Society in October 2004. There, an academic announced in a public lecture that human beings could live forever—by which he meant that within the next twenty-five years, medical science will possess the capacity to repair all known effects of aging. The average age at death of people born thereafter would exceed five thousand years.

In fact, those expecting significant breakthroughs in the treatment of disease (and significant profits by the large pharmaceutical companies) after the decoding of the human genome in 2001 were disappointed. The pharmaceutical industry was hesitant to invest in new products designed for conditions affecting small numbers of people. The fears associated with "personalized medicine" have begun to disappear, because it is obvious that there are generic processes from which genomics companies can profit. Genetics-based medicine is poised to find better diagnostic tests for and generic solutions to such conditions as diabetes, Alzheimer's disease, heart problems, and breast cancer. These advances will, without doubt, radically enhance life expectancy.

The human consequences of these changes will be rapid and radical, but little thought has been given to the social and political consequences of extended longevity. Although it is mere speculation, one can assume that a new pattern of aging would produce a range of major socioeconomic problems. Growing world inequality between the rejuvenated North and the naturally aging South would further inflame the resentment of deprived social groups against wealthy aged populations. The labor market would fail to cope with the increasing number of human survivors, and housing markets would face parallel crises. The food supply's inability to keep up with population expansion would increase economic dependency on genetically modified food. There would be additional environmental pollution, global warming, and further depletion of natural resources. Intergenerational conflicts over resources—including conflicts over jobs, retirement benefits, pensions, and housing—would be exacerbated. The rapid transformation of family structures would continue as the elderly survived in greater numbers, presumably taking on new partners and reproducing in new households through unlimited serial monogamy. The theological notion of an afterlife would probably disappear, as most survivors would literally experience eternal life or at least indefinite life on earth. Yet while genomic sciences could reduce mortality, we might assume that (at least in the short term) they would increase morbidity, with rising rates of chronic illness and geriatric diseases. Living forever would mean, in practice, living forever in a morbid condition. As surviving populations discovered new levels of boredom through the endless repetition of the same, there would be growing psychological problems, including depression, ennui, and despair, resulting periodically in bouts of collective hysteria and suicide.

The prospect of indefinite life would thus bring on an acute Malthusian crisis. These transformations imply an interesting change from early to late modernity. In the early stages of capitalism, the role of medical science was to improve health care, making the working class healthy in order to have an efficient labor force. Late capitalism does not need a large labor force at full employment and working full time, because technology has made labor more efficient. In the new biotechnological environment, disease is no longer a negative force in the economy; on the contrary, it is a factor of production.

CONCLUSION: SOVEREIGNTY, SECURITY, AND RIGHTS

The underlying logic of this chapter has been to defend the argument about vulnerability by showing that improvements in medical science and technology could not make human life significantly less vulnerable. The possibility of living forever has been employed to push the argument to its limits. The implications of this study of aging and longevity are that vulnerability defines what it is to be human. If vulnerability is the foundation of our humanity, then medical science can offer the prospect of a dystopian future in which human rights would no longer apply unambiguously to post-humans. Medical science threatens to erode our humanity—and to make our world more precarious by increasing social regulation or medicalization, often at the cost of civil liberties.

It is not conceivable that we could live forever. More realistically, if life expectancy in the advanced economies increased, say, by ten years in the next five years or by twenty years in the next decade through regenerative medicine, then the global consequences could be very damaging. These might include a major depletion of natural resources and an increase in the speed of environmental decline through increased industrialization, which would be necessary to support a rapid increase in the world's population. People living in the developing world would primarily experience the negative consequences. This economic and social crisis would result from our inability to find renewable energy.

Given Malthusian assumptions about scarcity, relatively fixed resources, and the entropy law, it follows that vulnerability and precariousness are inescapable features of human life. We thus need human rights to protect us from contingency. Yet it also follows that, for example, there must be limits to Article 3, in which "everyone has the right to life." It cannot be the case that I have a right to life indefinitely at somebody else's expense. This limitation points to the importance of the social dimension of rights: the exercise of rights must be to our collective advantage. Vulnerability is a collective condition, which can only be addressed or moderated within a shared world. While Malthusian conflict is probably the unavoidable feature of our times, human rights institutions hold out the modest collective promise of less violence and more security. Against the prospect of a medical utopia, this essay asserts that suffering is inevitable and misery is universal. These conditions can be regarded as the driving force behind all religious worldviews or cosmologies, insofar as religion is basically a theodicy— that is, an explanation of suffering. Through these conditions, then, our humanity is constituted (Wilkinson 2005). We suffer because we are vulnerable, and we need, above all else, institutions that will give us some degree of security.

7

OLD AND NEW XENOPHOBIA

INTRODUCTION: THE STRANGER

In *Of Hospitality* (2000), Jacques Derrida has written eloquently and convincingly about the rights of the stranger, arguing that ethics is in fact hospitality. His account of hospitality follows Émile Benveniste, who in *Indo-European Language and Society* (1973) demonstrated the ambiguous and contradictory nature of a cluster of concepts: host, guest, and stranger. In Latin, a stranger/guest is called *hostis* and *hospes*. Whereas *hospes* is the etymological root of "hospitality," *hostis* is an "enemy." Benveniste argued that both "guest" and "enemy" derive from "stranger," and the notion of "favorable stranger" evolved eventually into "guest," while a "hostile stranger" became the enemy. More precisely, the idea of a stranger in Latin is closely related to debates about rights and membership of the household. Whereas *peregrinus* was a category of person living (or peregrinating) outside the boundaries of a political territory, *hostis* referred to a stranger in the midst of the city who was recognized as enjoying equal rights with Roman citizens. In Latin, the *hostis* is always bound by a set of exchanges, or gifts, that create mutual obligation through reciprocity, but the problem is that gifts can also be competitive and aggressive. They compel as well as oblige, but the point of this argument is that *hostis*—unlike *peregrinus*—reflects a near, not distant, relationship. In the ancient world, a stranger is a person who lives in the neighborhood or vicinity and who can be bound to us by shared ritual activity.

The same issues are present in the Greek *xenos* (stranger), from which we derive "xenophobia." The term *xenos* indicated a pact involving definite obligations that could be inherited by subsequent generations. These *xenia,* or social contracts, came under the protection of Zeus Xenios and consisted of an exchange of gifts between the contracting parties, who thereby bound their descendants to the agreement. In ancient Greece, both kings and commoners could be bound by these pacts with (friendly) strangers. Yet with the growth of the state and the decline of the ancient world, these ritualized relationships between men (I use the gendered noun deliberately) and between clans were replaced by a new classification of what was inside and what was outside the *civitas.* In the terminology of modern political philosophy, these ritualized relationships were replaced by secular citizenship, which is a system of contributory rights and duties that bind people to the nation-state. Taxation replaces the system of gift-enforced relationships.

In European languages, we do not—according to the *Shorter Oxford English Dictionary*—possess a word parallel to xenophobia, such as "xenophilia." Within the Indo-European languages there is no apparent trace of xenophilia. This absence is telling. It seems that there is no linguistic possibility for the love of strangers; there is simply no social role for a stranger who can become an object of genuine friendship. We might conclude, therefore, that xenophobia is the normal state of affairs in the relationship between social groups.

We should, though, distinguish between "old xenophobia" and "new xenophobia." The former refers to a set of social circumstances that existed in ancient society before the rise of the modern state. In old xenophobia, the stranger as an enemy is a clearly recognized person who lives proximately, in our midst, or adjacent to our community. The traditional stranger is a palpable figure with whom we can exchange gifts. He can be welcomed to the fireplace, the foundation of the classical city, and he can accept with us the authority of the fireside gods. In particular, the stranger is somebody whom we can marry, or with whom we might exchange women. The exchange of gifts is typically institutionalized by strictly defined activities of gift giving. This reciprocal relationship is always ambiguous—a mixture of cooperative and threatening behavior, a relationship only partially regulated by ritual customs and practices. It can always break down into a hostile relationship or periodically into war. Warfare in ancient society, however, was itself typically ritualized behavior, not necessarily leading to the systematic extermination of the enemy. The stranger might become a domestic slave as a result of warfare; alternatively, after a series of skirmishes, more peaceful relations could be reestablished. Ethnic cleansing was not common in ancient societies, because such forms of organized extermination required considerable planning and coordination, namely, the involvement of the state and its administration. A holocaust is a modern strategy to eliminate a whole population, not a military strategy of warring bands.

These ancient relationships of *xenia* can be compared with modern circumstances. Citizens in modern states establish legal relationships with strangers by creating criteria of membership through various forms of naturalization. With the growth of states, a complex web of classificatory niches emerges, including stateless person, refugee, asylum seeker, guest worker, and migrant. Some states also recognize dual citizenship or classificatory schemes that, in effect, create "quasi-citizens." The logic of this political development is described by Saskia Sassen (1999) in her *Guests and Aliens*. The rise of the modern state brought to an end the traditional migratory routes of informal or casual workers who moved around Europe on a seasonal basis in search of part-time employment. These sojourns typically followed the migration of herring around northern Europe or corresponded with harvesting. By creating passports and strict membership based on citizenship, modern states converted such seasonal workers (or guests) into aliens who required passports or work permits to enter a national territory. While the transition from the ancient world to the nation-state created major changes in identity, there were continuities with the old world. Modern citizenship also implicitly involves a system of exchange, or what I have called contributory rights. The citizen is somebody who, through a series of contributions such as employment, public service, and parenting, enjoys a set of corresponding entitlements (to vote or to receive welfare benefits or social security). In principle, strangers can become part of this network of rights and duties, if they also begin to participate in the host society.

Yet these relationships between host and stranger, or between citizen and guest worker, have been transformed by globalization, and a new type of xenophobia has emerged. With globalization, especially the globalization of labor markets, modern societies have all become multicultural societies to some degree. And with the global development of diasporic communities, the stranger is both proximate and distant, because he (or she) is involved in a network of communities extending around the world. Migrant labor is typically connected to economically marginal societies or communities, and their remittances are often necessary to support distant communities. Where migrant laborers do not become integrated into the host community through marriage, work, or citizenship, they can remain isolated from the mainstream. Indeed, with some forms of multiculturalism, cultural differences become institutionalized and produce fragmented, isolated, and underprivileged social groups. Their children then become part of a marginalized urban underclass.

These migrant communities have been increasingly augmented by a flow of stateless people, refugees, asylum seekers, boat people, victims of failed states and civil wars, and the human flotsam and jetsam of new wars. The growth of global cities has also been accompanied by a global underclass of illegal or semi-legal migrants and refugees who work in the informal economy and come to constitute a "weight of the world" (Bourdieu 1993). The stranger becomes an anonymous and placeless person without citizenship or rights, a member of an underclass that is seen by the state to form a recruiting ground for criminals and terrorists. In the global economy, the stranger is recruited not to service in the formal economy of society but to a career in prisons, detention camps, inter-state zones, departure areas, and a variety of other intermediate, quasi-legal zones.

The stranger has become increasingly an international rather than merely a national problem. According to the Office of the United Nations High Commissioner for Refugees (UNHCR), the number of refugees crossing international borders has risen from 2.4 million in 1975 to 10.5 million in 1985 and to 14.4 million in 1995—but if we include internally displaced persons, then the total refugee figure is more like 38 million people. The number of displaced persons per conflict has risen from 40,000 per conflict in 1969 to 857,000 per conflict in 1992 (Kaldor 2001, 101). The stranger, who is the target of new xenophobia, is a displaced person. Typically these strangers are a woman and her children, seen as a weight on the local economy. They may indeed ultimately contribute to the collapse of local economies. These new strangers do not bear gifts for exchange, only burdens.

During the Cold War, Western states supported human rights (at the very least as an ideology compatible with Western notions of individualism). The contemporary war on terrorism has, however—since 9/11 and 7/7—turned many Western states against migration and hardened attitudes toward political refugees and stateless peoples. Governments now emphasize their responsibility toward citizens in terms of providing security, not defending rights. While sociologists have talked much about globalization and the erosion of the state, the modern security crisis has seen "the return of the state." The attack on the Twin Towers produced the USA PATRIOT Act in the United States and the Terrorism Act in the United Kingdom. This legislation has, for civil liberty campaigners, infringed individual liberties and increased the power of the state to arrest and deport suspected terrorists and criminals. The demand for greater security has justified greater surveillance of the population through phone tapping and the monitoring of the Web.

Yet the London bombings were not performed by outsiders. The aftermath of 7/7 is, at least for Europeans, more significant than 9/11, because the bombings and attempted bombings in London were undertaken by British citizens, the children of migrants and asylum seekers. In the new xenophobia, the "friendly stranger" is now the "hostile stranger," and every citizen has become a potential enemy within. The essential condition for the new xenophobia is a political situation in which the majority feels that it is under attack and that its way of life is threatened by social groups it does not understand, cannot identify, and consequently does not recognize. The threatened majority suspects that its own state protects strangers through liberal laws that allow criminal activities to flourish. The old rituals of hospitality toward the stranger who warms himself by the fireside have collapsed in the rubble of the Twin Towers.

Where there is low trust, there is a growing sense of the offensive nature of juvenile crime and vandalism, and this incivility is increasingly associated with migrant communities and their dislodged young men. As Abdelmalek Sayad (2004, 282) observes in his *Suffering of the Immigrant,* migration has produced a new "state thought" in which the criminality of the migrant has become ontological, "because, at the deepest level of our mode of thought (i.e., state thought) it is synonymous with the very existence of the immigrant and with the very fact of immigration." The stranger has become a free-floating, dangerous "guest" who emerges periodically to commit irrational crimes or monstrous and inhumane acts of terror. Whereas the old xenophobia was regulated by gift giving, cooperation, and ritual, the new xenophobia confronts the violent stranger whose behavior (random violence against civilian targets) appears to have no logic. The modern stranger has become *peregrinus*—that is, somebody whose peregrination is global, without anchor, without connections, and without responsibilities. The somewhat arcane noun "peregrinity" means something foreign, strange, and outlandish. The new xenophobia is thus a collective psychological response to peregrinity.

The modern state has a contradictory relationship to multiculturalism and migration, on the one hand, and to order and sovereignty, on the other. In a capitalist society, the state wants to encourage labor migration, porous boundaries, and minimal limitations on labor fluidity and flexibility. The state is under pressure from economic elites to reduce labor's resistance to the logic of capital accumulation, and one solution to this problem is to import labor. But the state also has an interest in its own sovereignty, and hence it wants to impose a cultural and moral unity on society. Its economic interests produce cultural diversity through labor migration, but its need to protect its sovereignty commits it to moral unity, to the reduction of cultural complexity, and to the assimilation of the migrant. The modern state is an administrative order that seeks to maximize the social potential of its population (and thus it has an interest in supporting migration), but it also has an interest in the enforcement of a particular type of governmentality. The state wants to maintain its political boundary against external heterogeneity to protect its sovereignty and to sustain porous economic borders in order to stimulate its economy to maintain its economic position in the world.

As a result of this contradiction, state policies toward citizenship and migration vacillate between treating migration and multiculturalism as aspects of economic policy and treating multiculturalism within a framework of asserting national sovereignty. Given the current climate of global conflict and uncertainty, modern states tend to give priority to security over welfare and to public order over civil liberties. In part, this situation explains the new emphasis on civic integration over multicultural difference. The modern state is increasingly committed to the notion that sovereignty resides in the capacity to make decisions in a situation of political emergency (Schmitt 1996).

CONDITIONS FOR MULTICULTURALISM

Multiculturalism can only be sustained where there are overlapping associational supports for diversity and where there is sufficient countervailing social cohesion to sustain the political tensions that arise from cultural complexity. We can divide these conditions into the economic, the cultural and educational, and, finally, the political and juridical.

Recent criticism of multiculturalism claims that the emphasis on difference and identity politics has submerged the importance of economic equality. So-called critical multiculturalism requires both mutual recognition and redistribution of national resources to create equality of the objective conditions of existence between host and migration societies (Hamilton 1996). The economic conditions for multiculturalism include rapid and sustained economic growth, a safety-net welfare state, and some redistribution of wealth through a progressive tax system. Perhaps the hallmark of citizenship is, in fact, a shared taxation system and low levels of tax avoidance. These economic conditions will never in themselves be sufficient, however. In this respect, the multicultural record of social democratic societies such as Denmark and Sweden is not particularly encouraging (Craig 2002; Kamali 1997). There must be a direct confrontation with racism and racist ideologies in addition to the development of successful social policies.

The main plank of successful multiculturalism must be the creation of overlapping social and cultural ties to create social bonds and social capital between groups. One of the critical issues in cultural recognition is the question of gender, and this issue is reflected in and measured by rates of interfaith marriage. Generally speaking, there is no solution to this problem, as most religious groups encourage or prescribe intra-faith marriages. Issues surrounding gender equality, intercommunal marriage, female education, the veil, seclusion, clitoridectomy, and circumcision remain the most divisive aspects of the debate about multiculturalism. This conflict is not just about Islam but about all faith-based communities. The situation is probably getting worse rather than better as religion increasingly serves as the basis of modern identity and the mechanism for political mobilization. The notion that individuals can opt out of their own communities, religious or otherwise, is highly problematic. In the case of minorities, the survival of their cultures and traditions requires continuity of socialization and transmission—a process that has historically depended on women. Hence, women are typically subject to excessive (and at times brutal) subordination to group norms. This sociological fact, though, offers no normative reason to support gender inequalities.

To some extent, state educational systems that (in principle) provide children with intercultural experiences, promote a positive view of multiculturalism, and encourage cosmopolitanism can only be partially successful when the home experience is monocultural and outside the mainstream of multiculturalism. In Britain, when the state started to support Catholic schools, there was counterintuitively greater inclusion of Catholics into mainstream politics. Following this example, the state has diverted public funds to support Muslim schools, but it is not self-evident that Muslims will as a result be more fully incorporated into civil society. Separate Muslim education is, in part, designed to segregate and seclude Muslim girls in order to ensure that they marry within the community. Yet one cannot blame these private schools, as the publicly funded state schools have hardly done better. In a speech to the Manchester Council for Community Relations in 2005, Trevor Phillips, chief of the Commission for Racial Equality, cited the case of Tower Hamlets in London, where seventeen primary state schools had over 90 percent Bangladeshi pupils, while another nine schools had only 10 percent. Among the fifteen secondary schools, two schools had over 95 percent of their students coming from the Bangladeshi community. British schools in inner London have therefore an implicit apartheid, largely along racial lines.

The cultural argument for multiculturalism is that the national community can only be bound together by shared values. We might call these shared values an ideology, but clearly nationalism has been the powerful social glue in the United States, Canada, and Australia in binding diverse groups together. National sports might also act as a cultural supplement to a nationalist ideology, a shared welfare state, and a common schooling experience. The spectacle of national success in international games might have the beneficial effect of creating social solidarity. With the game of cricket, there is a multicultural global community that transcends ethic conflict—including between India and Pakistan, or between India and Sri Lanka. Unfortunately, there are probably as many counterexamples as there are supporting cases. English soccer has been an important recruiting ground for fascist youth groups and those subscribing to racist politics in Britain, Holland, Denmark, and Germany. The conflicts between Turkish and English soccer teams have not offered encouraging signs of cosmopolitanism.

In the absence of a compensating nationalist ideology, shared schooling, and a common language, societies have to rely increasingly on political and juridical solutions. There must be governmental policies that promote tolerance and understanding—namely, a set of government measures that seem to support "cosmopolitan virtue." There should also be provision of relatively modest criteria of naturalization and access to full citizenship. In this respect, Australia has been far more generous and open than either Britain or Germany. The rate of naturalization, therefore, can be used as an objective measure of multicultural openness (Brubaker 1992). The critical bedrock of multiculturalism must, however, be the rule of law and procedural guarantees of judicial fairness. Multicultural societies are unlikely to achieve agreement about substantive issues of law and justice, but at least they may agree about juridical transparency and procedural norms.

Numerous conditions undermine multiculturalism. They include, as a minimum, situations in which governments seem to take sides in ethnic conflict and appear to promote the interests of one group over another. Communal hostilities are then fueled because the rule of law is overtly flaunted. Ethnic conflict creates conditions for the development of civil strife, and civil strife can lead ultimately to new wars. The lack of intermarriage sustains civil distrust, and the prohibition on intermarriage is typically upheld by fundamentalist religions. Finally, economic circumstances contribute to conflict, especially high levels of unemployment, low wages, and exploitative working conditions. These circumstances make it difficult for young people to benefit from secular citizenship and make militant or militaristic alternatives look attractive. Such forms of social and cultural alienation breed social conflict, civil disorder, and terrorism.

New wars produce growing social incivility, and they are one important cause of the global increase in homeless and stateless peoples. Refugee camps and other transitional zones produce conditions within which terrorism and criminality can flourish. They create a global network of drug trafficking, slavery, and illegal arms sales. Given modern interconnectivity, new wars have the general consequence of destabilizing civil society. Insofar as new wars contribute to failed states, they have an important impact on human rights abuse. They fuel the spread of new xenophobia, and they make multicultural values and cosmopolitan virtue difficult to nurture and sustain. These considerations lead to the argument that we are faced by a stark choice between cosmopolitanism and nihilism, between humane values and xenophobic hatred, between multiculturalism and racism.

CONCLUSION: THE END OF MULTICULTURALISM?

According to Thomas Hobbes's theory of the state, we can only achieve some degree of personal security if we surrender a modicum of our own freedom in order to establish the state's sovereignty. Herein is the great intellectual puzzle of political science, because politics can never be wholly universal; it is essentially about the struggle for resources between conflicting groups whose motivation is to achieve power. Politics involves a contradiction between the state—which needs to achieve some level of legitimacy in order to function—and the struggle for power that appears to take place outside the framework of law, which is necessary for the continuity of the state. The legitimacy of the modern state is tied to the provision of security for its citizens. There appears to be an irreconcilable tension between any universal human rights regime and the legitimacy of the state, which is particular and exclusive. Yet this tension between the state and citizenship, on the one hand, and global governance and human rights, on the other, may turn out to be deceptive.

In the course of my writing this book, bombings in Istanbul, Madrid, London, and Bali have shaped the more general public debate about the nature of terrorism, human rights, and the role of the state. The American and British governments have been anxious to change the law, which is often seen to be unduly generous in protecting the civil liberties of individuals and groups whose beliefs appear hostile to Western liberal culture. In these circumstances, there is little room for optimism, and the idea of cosmopolitanism often appears to be out of step with public opinion. Accusations that the Bush administration has condoned extensive phone tapping domestically and has used secret detention centers around the world to interrogate suspects without any consideration for due process indicate a grey area between legal and illegal activity in the war on terror. In these circumstances, what is the difference between terrorist violence and counterterrorism measures? The coercive force available to the state is legitimate if it is subordinate to legal norms, that is, to the rule of law. State violence is legitimate only as a last resort or a lesser evil (Ignatieff 2004)—only if it is ultimately restrained and made accountable as a consequence of the due process of law. In the twentieth century, the legitimacy of the state came to depend increasingly on the extent to which both domestic and foreign policy of powerful states were compatible with international human rights standards. The legal difficulty for the coalition forces in Iraq has been that the original invasion and subsequent treatment of prisoners do not appear to be consistent with UN requirements or human rights objectives. The notion that terrorism creates exceptional circumstances that permit states to act outside human rights norms is likely to be counterproductive. Such actions merely give further credibility to terrorist ideologies and continue to erode the UN's authority.

Human vulnerability sits, therefore, at the heart of human rights principles, because security is a necessary condition for containing our vulnerability, and legality and legitimacy are preconditions of human security. The political world has become increasingly precarious, and the contemporary international crisis is not well served by academic arguments supporting moral relativism. Recognizing our common vulnerability is the only starting point for the construction of a commonwealth in which security might be restored.

The social and economic conditions for multiculturalism will include sustained economic growth and opportunities for social mobility, especially for minority groups; a national, secular education system that contributes to social mobility and integrates children of different ethnic and religious traditions; freedom to choose marriage partners, high rates of intermarriage, and liberal divorce laws; and, finally, the rule of law and a government that is overtly committed to policies supporting multiculturalism. The social causes for failed multicultural diversity are the obverse: declining economic growth and social inequality, where stigmatized minority communities find fewer opportunities for social mobility; a low level of cross-cultural marriage; segregated educational systems; and governments that actively intervene in society to the disadvantage of minority communities. Multiculturalism fails because social conditions undermine trust and social cohesion. Indeed, the conditions that produce trust are being eroded as social capital declines with the dominance of egoistic individualism.

We should distinguish between multiculturalism as a policy, as a state of affairs, and as an ideal. Multicultural policies are being abandoned in many liberal societies. Multiculturalism itself, though, is an unavoidable state of affairs. Yet multiculturalism also implies a moral standpoint, one in which respect and mutual recognition can create a platform for diverse but prosperous and successful societies. While multiculturalism may be under siege, the main choice is not between multiculturalism and monoculturalism, but between cosmopolitanism and nihilism.

I conclude this study with a quotation from the American black intellectual Cornel West. Pondering the condition of black Americans in his *Race Matters* (1993, 8), West commented that to "establish a new framework, we need to begin with a frank acknowledgement of the basic humanness and Americanness of each of us. And we must acknowledge that as a people—*E Pluribus Unum*—we are on a slippery slope toward economic strife, social turmoil, and cultural chaos. If we go down, we go down together." The same could be said for our contemporary global condition. While current policies of multiculturalism may be under attack, and while some policies may have failed miserably, we cannot avoid a multicultural and cosmopolitan future in which citizenship and human rights will be our best defense against going down together—possibly indefinitely.

REFERENCES

Ahmed, L. 1992. *Women and Gender in Islam.* New Haven: Yale University Press.

Albrecht, G. 1992. *The Disability Business.* London: Sage.

Alexopoulos, G. 2003. *Stalin's Outcasts: Aliens, Citizens, and the Soviet State, 1926–1936.* Ithaca: Cornell University Press.

Alter, J. S. 2000. *Gandhi's Body: Sex, Diet, and the Politics of Nationalism.* Philadelphia: University of Pennsylvania Press.

Anwar, Z. 2001. "What Islam, Whose Islam? Sisters in Islam and the Struggle for Women's Rights." In *The Politics of Multiculturalism: Pluralism and Citizenship in Malaysia, Singapore, and Indonesia,* ed. R. W. Heffner, 227–52. Honolulu: University of Hawai'i Press.

Arendt, H. 1951. *The Origins of Totalitarianism.* New York: Harcourt Brace.

———. 1963. *Eichmann in Jerusalem: A Report on the Banality of Evil.* New York: Viking Press.

———. 2003. *Responsibility and Judgment.* New York: Schocken Books.

Bader, V. 1999. "For Love of Country." *Political Theory* 27 (3): 379–97.

Bales, K. 1999. *Disposable People: New Slavery in the Global Economy.* Berkeley and Los Angeles: University of California Press.

———. 2004. "Slavery and the Human Right to Evil." *Journal of Human Rights* 3 (1): 55–65.

Barbalet, J. M. 1998. *Emotion, Social Theory, and Social Structure: A Macrosociological Approach.* Cambridge: Cambridge University Press.

Barnes, C., G. Mercer, and T. Shakespeare. 1999. *Exploring Disability.* Cambridge: Polity Press.

Bauman, Z. 1989. *Modernity and the Holocaust.* Cambridge: Polity Press.

Beck, U. 2000. *What Is Globalization?* Cambridge: Polity Press.

Beck, U., and Beck-Gernsheim, E. 1995. *The Normal Chaos of Love.* Cambridge: Polity Press.

Bell, D., and J. Binnie. 2000. *The Sexual Citizen: Queer Politics and Beyond.* Cambridge: Polity Press.

Bendix, R. 1964. *Nation-Building and Citizenship: Studies of Our Changing Social Order.* New York: John Wiley and Sons.

Benveniste, É. 1973. *Indo-European Language and Society.* Coral Gables, Fla.: University of Miami Press.

Berger, P. L. 1967. *The Sacred Canopy.* New York: Doubleday.

Berger, P. L., and T. Luckmann. 1967. *The Social Construction of Reality.* New York: Doubleday.

Berger, P. L., and H. Kellner. 1965. "Arnold Gehlen and the Theory of Institutions." *Social Research* 32 (1): 110–15.

Berlin, I. 1969. *Four Essays on Liberty.* Oxford: Oxford University Press.

———. 1978. *Karl Marx: His Life and Environment.* Oxford: Oxford University Press.

Bickenbach, J. E. 2001. "Disability Human Rights, Law, and Policy." In *Handbook of Disability Studies,* ed. G. L. Albrecht, K. D. Seelman, and M. Bury, 565–84. London: Sage.

Bobbio, N., and M. Viroli. 2003. *The Idea of the Republic.* Cambridge: Polity Press.

Bourdieu, P., ed. 1993. *La misère du monde.* Paris: Seuil.

———. 2000. *Pascalian Meditations.* Cambridge: Polity Press.

Brubaker, W. R. 1992. *Citizenship and Nationhood in France and Germany.* Cambridge, Mass.: Harvard University Press.

Cabezas, A. L. 2002. "Tourism, Sex Work, and Women's Rights in the Dominican Republic." In *Globalization and Human Rights,* ed. A. Brysk, 44–60. Berkeley and Los Angeles: University of California Press.

Cohen, S. 2001. *States of Denial: Knowing about Atrocities and Suffering.* Cambridge: Polity Press.

Coleman, J. S. 1990. *Foundations of Social Theory.* Cambridge, Mass.: Harvard University Press.

Cooke, M. 1997. "Authenticity and Autonomy: Taylor, Habermas, and the Politics of Recognition." *Political Theory* 25 (2): 258–88.

Cowan, J. K., M-B. Dembour, and R. A. Wilson, eds. 2001. *Culture and Rights: Anthropological Perspectives.* Cambridge: Cambridge University Press.

Craig, G. 2002. "Ethnicity, Racism, and the Labour Market: A European Perspective." In *Changing Labour Markets, Welfare Policies, and Citizenship,* ed. J. G. Andersen and P. H. Jensen, 149–82. Bristol: Policy Press.

Deflem, M., ed. 1996. *Habermas, Modernity, and Law.* London: Sage.

Derrida, J. 2000. *Of Hospitality.* Stanford: Stanford University Press.

Deveaux, M. 2000. *Cultural Pluralism and Dilemmas of Justice.* Ithaca: Cornell University Press.

De Waal, A. 2003. "Human Rights Organizations and the Political Imagination: How the West and Africa Have Diverged." *Journal of Human Rights* 2 (4): 475–94.

Dubos, R. 1960. *The Mirage of Health.* London: Allen and Unwin.

Durkheim, É. 1992. *Professional Ethics and Civic Morals.* London: Routledge and Kegan Paul.

Elias, N. 2000. *The Civilizing Process.* Oxford: Blackwell.

Ferguson, N. 2003. *Empire: How Britain Made the Modern World.* London: Allen Lane.

Foucault, M. 1970. *The Order of Things.* London: Tavistock.

———. 1971. *Madness and Civilization.* London: Tavistock.

———. 1991. "Governmentality." In *The Foucault Effect,* ed. G. Burchell, C. Gordon, and P. Miller, 87–104. London: Harvester Wheatsheaf.

Fraser, N. 2001. "Recognition Without Ethics." *Theory, Culture, and Society* 18 (2–3): 21–42.

Fukuyama, F. 2002. *Our Posthuman Future: Consequences of the Biotechnological Revolution.* New York: Farrar, Straus and Giroux.

Gehlen, A. 1988. *Man: His Nature and Place in the World.* New York: Columbia University Press.

Georgescu-Roegen, N. 1971. *The Entropy Law and the Economic Process.* Cambridge, Mass.: Harvard University Press.

Glazer, N. 1997. *We Are All Multiculturalists Now.* Cambridge, Mass.: Harvard University Press.

———. 2002. "Dual Citizenship as a Challenge to Sovereignty." In *Sovereignty under Challenge: How Governments Respond,* ed. J. D. Montgomery and N. Glazer, 33–54. New Brunswick: Transaction Books.

Goffman, E. 1961. *Asylums.* Harmondsworth: Penguin Books.

Habermas, J. 1987. *The Philosophical Discourse of Modernity.* Cambridge: Polity Press.

———. 1989. *The Structural Transformation of the Public Sphere: An Inquiry into a Category of Bourgeois Society.* Cambridge, Mass.: MIT Press.

———. 1990. *Moral Consciousness and Communicative Action.* Cambridge: Polity Press.

———. 1997. *Between Facts and Norms.* Cambridge: Polity Press.

Haeri, S. 1989. *Law of Desire: Temporary Marriage in Iran.* London: I. B. Tauris.

Hamilton, C. 1996. "Multiculturalism as a Political Strategy." In *Mapping Multiculturalism,* ed. A. Gordon and C. Newfield, 167–76. Minneapolis: University of Minnesota Press.

Hayflick, L. 1982. "Biological Aspects of Aging." In *Biological and Social Aspects of Mortality and the Length of Life,* ed. S. H. Preston, 223–58. Liège: Ordina.

Heidegger, M. 1962. *Being and Time.* Oxford: Blackwell.

Hirst, P. 2001. *War and Power in the Twenty-first Century: The State, Military Conflict, and the International System.* Cambridge: Polity Press.

Hunt, A. 1978. *The Sociological Movement in Law.* London: Macmillan.

Huxley, A. 1998. *Brave New World.* New York: Perennial Classics.

Ignatieff, M. 2001. *Human Rights as Politics and Idolatry.* Princeton: Princeton University Press.

———. 2004. *The Lesser Evil: Political Ethics in an Age of Terror.* Princeton: Princeton University Press.

Joas, H. 2003. *War and Modernity.* Cambridge: Polity Press.

Joppke, C. 2004. "The Retreat of Multiculturalism in the Liberal State: Theory and Policy." *British Journal of Sociology* 55 (2): 237–57.

Juergensmeyer, M. 2000. *Terror in the Mind of God: The Global Rise of Religious Violence.* Berkeley and Los Angeles: University of California Press.

Kaldor, M. 2001. *New and Old Wars: Organized Violence in a Global Era.* Cambridge: Polity Press.

Kamali, M. 1997. *Distorted Integration: Clientization of Immigrants in Sweden.* Uppsala: Uppsala Multiethnic Papers.

Kass, L. R. 2002. *Life, Liberty, and the Defense of Dignity: The Challenge for Bioethics.* San Francisco: Encounter Books.

Keay, D. 1987. "AIDS, Education, and the Year 2000" (interview with Margaret Thatcher). *Woman's Own* (October 31): 8–10.

Kepel, G. 2002. *Jihad: The Trail of Political Islam.* London: I. B. Tauris.

Kramer, P. D. 1994. *Listening to Prozac.* London: Fourth Estate.

Kukathas, C. 1992a. "Are There Any Cultural Rights?" *Political Theory* 20:105–39.

———. 1992b. "Cultural Rights Again." *Political Theory* 20:674–80.

Kymlicka, W. 1995. *Multicultural Citizenship.* Oxford: Oxford University Press.

Ledgerwood, J. L., and K. Un. 2003. "Global Concepts and Local Meaning: Human Rights and Buddhism in Cambodia." *Journal of Human Rights* 2 (4): 531–49.

Ling, T. 1973. *The Buddha.* New York: Charles Scribner's Sons.

Locke, J. 1960. *Two Treatises on Government.* Cambridge: Cambridge University Press.

Lotka, A. J. 1925. *Elements of Physical Biology.* Baltimore: Williams and Wilkins.

Mandaville, P. 2001. *Transnational Muslim Politics.* London: Routledge.

Marshall, T. H. 1950. *Citizenship and Social Class and Other Essays.* Cambridge: Cambridge University Press.

Mommsen, W. J. 1984. *Max Weber and German Politics, 1890–1920.* Chicago: University of Chicago Press.

Montgomery, H. 2001. "Imposing Rights? A Case Study of Child Prostitution in Thailand." In *Culture and Rights: Anthropological Perspectives,* ed. J. K.

Cowan, M-B. Dembour, and R. A. Wilson, 80–101. Cambridge: Cambridge University Press.

Montgomery, J. D., and N. Glazer, eds. 2002. *Sovereignty under Challenge*. New Brunswick: Transaction Books.

Moore, B., Jr. 1970. *Reflections on the Causes of Human Misery and upon Certain Proposals to Eliminate Them*. London: Allen Lane.

Münkler, H. 2005. *The New Wars*. Cambridge: Polity Press.

Nussbaum, M. 2000. *Women and Human Development: The Capabilities Approach*. Cambridge: Cambridge University Press.

———. 2001. *The Fragility of Goodness: Luck and Ethics in Greek Tragedy and Philosophy*. Cambridge: Cambridge University Press.

Ong, A. 1999. *Flexible Citizenship: The Cultural Logics of Transnationality*. Durham, N.C.: Duke University Press.

———. 2004. "Citizenship." In *A Companion to the Anthropology of Politics*, ed. D. Nugent and J. Vincent, 55–68. Oxford: Blackwell.

Orwell, G. 1937. *The Road to Wigan Pier*. London: Victor Gollancz.

———. 1949. *Nineteen Eighty-four*. London: Secker and Warburg.

Parsons, T., and K. Clark, eds. 1966. *The American Negro*. Boston: Houghton Mifflin.

Perkins, F. 2004. *Leibniz and China: A Commerce of Light*. Cambridge: Cambridge University Press.

Pogge, T. 2002. *World Poverty and Human Rights*. Cambridge: Polity Press.

Rawls, J. 1971. *A Theory of Justice*. London: Oxford University Press.

Richardson, D., and S. Seidman, eds. 2002. *Handbook of Gay and Lesbian Studies*. London: Sage.

Riesman, D. 1950. *The Lonely Crowd: A Study of the Changing American Character*. New Haven, Conn.: Yale University Press.

Ritzer, G. 2003. *Globalization of Nothing*. London: Sage.

Robertson, G. 2002. *Crimes Against Humanity: The Struggle for Global Justice*. New York: The New Press.

Robertson, R. 1992. *Globalization: Social Theory and Global Culture*. London: Sage.

———. 1995. "Glocalization: Time-Space and Homogeneity-Heterogeneity." In *Global Modernities*, ed. M. Featherstone, S. Lash, and R. Robertson, 25–44. London: Sage.

Rorty, R. 1989. *Contingency, Irony, and Solidarity*. Cambridge: Cambridge University Press.

———. 1998. *Achieving Our Nation: Leftist Thought in Twentieth-Century America*. Cambridge, Mass.: Harvard University Press.

Roy, O. 2004. *Globalised Islam: The Search for a New Ummah*. London: Hurst.

Sassen, S. 1999. *Guests and Aliens*. New York: The New Press.

Sayad, A. 2004. *The Suffering of the Immigrant*. Cambridge: Polity Press.

Scarry, E. 1985. *The Body in Pain: The Making and Unmaking of the World.* Oxford: Oxford University Press.

Schmitt, C. 1996. *The Concept of the Political.* Chicago: University of Chicago Press.

Schopenhauer, A. 2004. *On the Suffering of the World.* London: Penguin Books.

Shaw, M. 2003. *War and Genocide: Organized Killing in Modern Society.* Cambridge: Polity Press.

Shklar, J. N. 1998. *Redeeming American Political Thought.* Chicago: University of Chicago Press.

Shostak, S. 2002. *Becoming Immortal: Combining Cloning and Stem-Cell Therapy.* Albany: State University of New York Press.

Strauss, L. 1950. *Natural Right and History.* Chicago: University of Chicago Press.

Taylor, C. 1975. *Hegel.* Cambridge: Cambridge University Press.

———. 1992. *Multiculturalism and the Politics of Recognition.* Princeton: Princeton University Press.

———, ed. 1994. *Multiculturalism: Examining the Politics of Recognition.* Princeton: Princeton University Press.

———. 1999. "Conditions of an Unforced Consensus on Human Rights." In *The East Asian Challenge of Human Rights,* ed. J. R. Bauer and D. A. Bell, 124–44. Cambridge: Cambridge University Press.

Theweleit, K. 1987. *Male Fantasies.* Minneapolis: University of Minnesota Press.

Titmuss, R. 1962. *Income Distribution and Social Change.* London: Allen and Unwin.

Turner, B. S. 1984. *The Body and Society.* Oxford: Blackwell.

———. 1993. "Outline of a General Theory of Human Rights." *Sociology* 27 (3): 489–512.

———. 1998. "Forgetfulness and Frailty: Otherness and Rights in Contemporary Social Theory." In *The Politics of Jean-Francois Lyotard,* ed. C. Rojek and B. Turner, 25–42. London: Routledge.

———. 1999. "Citizenship and Health as a Scarce Resource." In *Second Opinion: An Introduction to Health Sociology,* ed. John Germov, 302–14. Oxford: Oxford University Press.

———. 2000. "Cosmopolitan Virtue: Loyalty and the City." In *Democracy, Citizenship, and the Global City,* ed. E. F. Isin, 129–47. London: Routledge.

———. 2001a. "Cosmopolitan Virtue: On Religion in a Global Age." *European Journal of Social Theory* 4 (2): 131–52.

———. 2001b. "The Erosion of Citizenship." *The British Journal of Sociology* 52 (2): 189–209.

————. 2001c. "Outline of a General Theory of Cultural Citizenship." In *Culture and Citizenship*, ed. N. Stevenson, 11–32. London: Sage.

————. 2002. "Cosmopolitan Virtue: Globalization and Patriotism." *Theory, Culture, and Society* 19 (1–2): 45–64.

————. 2003. "Biology, Vulnerability, and Politics." In *Debating Biology: Sociological Reflections on Health, Medicine, and Society*, ed. S. J. Williams, L. Birke, and G. A. Bendalow, 271–82. London: Routledge.

————. 2004. *The New Medical Sociology*. New York: Norton.

Turner, B. S., and C. Rojek. 2002. *Society and Culture: Principles of Scarcity and Solidarity*. London: Sage.

Viroli, M. 1995. *For Love of Country: An Essay on Patriotism and Nationalism*. Oxford: Clarendon Press.

Weber, M. 1949. *The Methodology of the Social Sciences*. New York: Free Press.

————. 2002. *The Protestant Ethic and the Spirit of Capitalism*. London: Penguin Books.

Weinberg, D. 2005. *Of Others Inside: Insanity, Addiction, and Belonging in America*. Philadelphia: Temple University Press.

West, C. 1993. *Race Matters*. New York: Vintage Books.

Wilkinson, I. 2005. *Suffering: A Sociological Introduction*. Cambridge: Polity Press.

Williams, R. R. 1997. *Hegel's Ethics of Recognition*. Berkeley and Los Angeles: University of California Press.

Woodiwiss, A. 1998. *Globalisation, Human Rights, and Labour Law in Pacific Asia*. Cambridge: Cambridge University Press.

————. 2003. *Making Human Rights Work Globally*. London: Glasshouse Press.

————. 2005. *Human Rights*. London: Routledge.

INDEX